Homiletic Meditations Cycle C

The Day Of Pentecost
Through The Feast Of
Christ The King

Gospel
The Divine Advocacy
By Maurice A. Fetty

* * *

Gospel
Troubled Journey
By John G. Lynch

* * *

Gospel
Extraordinary Faith For Ordinary Time
By Larry R. Kalajainen

CSS Publishing Company, Inc.
Lima, Ohio

HOMILETIC MEDITATIONS — CYCLE C
THE DIVINE ADVOCACY
TROUBLED JOURNEY
EXTRAORDINARY FAITIH FOR ORDINARY TIME

Copyright © 1994 by
The CSS Publishing Company, Inc.
Lima, Ohio

All rights reserved. No part of this publication may be reproduced, stored in a retrieval system, or transmitted in any form or by any means, electronic, mechanical, photocopying, recording, or otherwise, without the prior permission of the publisher. Inquiries should be addressed to: The CSS Publishing Company, Inc., 517 South Main Street, P.O. Box 4503, Lima, Ohio 45802-4503.

Scripture quotations are from the *New Revised Standard Version of the Bible,* copyright 1989 by the Division of Christian Education of the National Council of the Churches of Christ in the USA. Used by permission.

Library of Congress Cataloging-in-Publication Data

Homiletic meditations.
   p.   cm.
   Contents: v. 1. Advent through the Transfiguration of Our Lord, first reading and Gospel, cycle C / Charles H. Bayer, Robert A. Hausman — v. 2. Lent through Ascension of Our Lord, first reading and Gospel texts, cycle C / Glenn Ludwig, Rodney T. Smothers — v. 3. Pentecost through the Feast of Christ the King, Gospel texts, cycle C / Maurice Fetty, John Lynch, Larry Kalajainen.
   ISBN 0-7880-0050-0 (v. 1). — ISBN 0-7880-0055-1 (v. 2). — ISBN 0-7880-0060-8 (v. 3).
   1. Church year sermons. 2. Bible. N.T. Gospels — Sermons. 3. Sermons, American. 4. Church year meditations.
BV4241.H565   1994
252'.6—dc20   94-207
                                                                                                           CIP

This book is available in the following formats, listed by ISBN:
0-7880-0060-8 Book
0-7880-0061-6 IBM (3 1/2 and 5 1/4) computer disk
0-7880-0062-4 IBM book and disk package
0-7880-0063-2 Macintosh computer disk
0-7880-0064-0 Macintosh book and disk package

Table Of Contents — Gospel

The Divine Advocacy

Pentecost — 11
People With Power To Forgive
John 20:19-23

The Holy Trinity — 19
The Divine Advocacy
John 16:12-15

Corpus Christi — 27
Five Thousand For Lunch In Galilee
Luke 9:11-17

Ordinary Time 9 — 35
Finding Faith In Unlikely People
Luke 7:1-10

Ordinary Time 10 — 45
How To Rise Above Discouragement
Luke 7:11-17

Ordinary Time 11 — 53
Dinner Parties With A Difference
Luke 7:36-50

Ordinary Time 12 — 61
Demons, Pigs And The Economy
Luke 8:26-39

Ordinary Time 13 69
   A New Kingdom Coming
   Luke 9:51-62

Ordinary Time 14 79
   How To Get The Job Done
   Luke 10:1-12

Ordinary Time 15 87
   The Persistent Noise Of Solemn Assemblies
   Luke 10:25-37

Table Of Contents — Gospel

Troubled Journey

Foreword	101
Introduction	103
Ordinary Time 16 The Better Part Luke 10:38-42	105
Ordinary Time 17 When Did Jesus Pray? Luke 11:1-13	109
Ordinary Time 18 Rich Toward God Luke 12:13-21	113
Ordinary Time 19 Fearful Flock Luke 12:32-48	117
Ordinary Time 20 Fire Word Luke 12:49-53	121
Ordinary Time 21 The Narrow Gate Luke 13:22-30	125

Ordinary Time 22   **129**
   Hold Your Peace?
   Luke 14:1, 7-14

Ordinary Time 23   **133**
   Hate Your Mother And Father?
   Luke 14:25-33

Ordinary Time 24   **137**
   The Other Ninety-nine
   Luke 15:1-10

Ordinary Time 25   **141**
   Ashamed To Beg
   Luke 16:1-13

Ordinary Time 26   **145**
   Desires Bring Hope
   Luke 16:19-31

Ordinary Time 27   **149**
   Millstones And Mustard Seeds
   Luke 17:5-10

Table Of Contents — Gospel

Extraordinary Faith For Ordinary Time

Introduction   155

Ordinary Time 28   159
    The Saving Power Of Gratitude
    Luke 17:11-19

Ordinary Time 29   167
    Tough Faith In Tough Times
    Luke 18:1-8

Ordinary Time 30   173
    The Good, The Bad And The Justified
    Luke 18:9-14

Ordinary Time 31   181
    Out On A Limb
    Luke 19:1-10

Feast Of All Saints   189
    Remembering The Saints
    Matthew 5:1-12

Ordinary Time 32   197
    The Importance Of Asking The Right Questions
    Luke 20:27-38

Ordinary Time 33   **205**
   Not Yet Quitting Time
   Luke 21:5-19

Thanksgiving Day   **213**
   The Bread That Endures
   Luke 17:11-19

The Feast Of Christ The King   **219**
   Pleased To Reconcile
   Luke 23:35-43

The Divine Advocacy

Maurice A. Fetty

Pentecost
John 20:19-23

People With Power To Forgive

Jesus began his earthly ministry preaching, teaching, healing and forgiving sins. And now at the end of his earthly ministry in his post-resurrection appearance to his disciples, Jesus is passing on to his disciples the ministry of preaching, teaching, healing and forgiving sins. Through the gift of the Holy spirit they are to be empowered to continue the work he inaugurated.

We often overlook in the gospels the connection between forgiveness and healing — healing that is both physical and spiritual. Consider, for example, the story of Jesus' healing the paralytic who was lowered through a roof to the feet of Jesus.

I have long enjoyed this story of Jesus' healing of the paralytic. It has drama to it, a deep sense of faith and friendship and a touch of humor. Think of it, a crowded house with people hanging out the windows and doors, so anxious were they to hear Jesus. (We latter-day disciples have always been amazed at Jesus' power to gather a crowd!)

And then there is the beautiful picture of the four men carrying their paralytic friend on a stretcher, attempting to get close to Jesus for healing. But the only way they possibly could get through that crowd was to go over them, something like a fullback at the goal line. So they went up the outside stairs to the roof, tore the roof apart and lowered the paralytic right in front of Jesus. Talk about determination and persistence!

But also talk about gall. Just who were they to think they could tear somebody's house apart? Can you see the debris and dust tumbling down? And then the paralytic being lowered, perhaps a little embarrassed? And can you see the owner of the house thinking, "Oh my gosh, there goes my roof. I wonder how much it will cost to repair." No doubt the local roofing contractor was smiling, already making out an estimate in his head!

Nevertheless, it is a charming story, a powerful story. It is a story of the faith and determination of four friends to try their best to get their friend to Jesus for healing. Where do you find friends like that today who care enough to put themselves out and to suffer embarrassment and inconvenience for the sake of someone else?

It is also a story which goes to a central problem of human existence — the problem of forgiveness. Is forgiveness possible? Are healing and forgiveness inter-related? Is religion more a hindrance than a help when it comes to forgiveness? And who is it, really, that has power to forgive sins?

It is well-known that in Jesus' time disease was often thought to be the result of sin. Following much the same theology as expressed in the book of Job, disease and misfortune were regarded as God's punishment for some wrong. On another occasion when Jesus healed the man born blind, the question was asked, "Who sinned, this man or his parents?" It was assumed that the blindness was a punishment for sin.

Addressing the popular thinking, Jesus said to the paralytic, "Man, your sins are forgiven you." The theologians, who had been sent from Jerusalem as a fact-finding team, accused him of blasphemy, claiming only God had power to forgive sins. More than that, God forgave people only after they had done enough acts of penance to deserve forgiveness.

Who did Jesus think he was, anyway? Was he presuming to be God? Jesus replied, "Well, would it be easier to say you are cured. Take up your bed and walk," which is precisely what the ex-paralytic did. The one who had been borne on the stretcher now was bearing it. The Son of Man does have power to forgive sins, and the cure is the proof of it, said Jesus.

Forgiveness is real. Forgiveness is possible, not only for God, but for the Son of Man, and the sons and daughters of men. Because we have received the Holy Spirit, we are all people with power to forgive. And we all are people with power to effect healing in our community. "If you forgive the sins of any, they are forgiven ..." said Jesus.

People have trouble with forgiveness because forgiveness implies judgment.

I remember some years ago encountering some super-religious types who announced that they were there to forgive me. Since I hardly knew them it felt like the familiar line we so much dread, "We're from the government, and we're here to help you." Most of us agree it is the kind of help we can do without. Likewise, I felt the forgiveness of those strangers was the kind of presumptuous forgiveness I could do without. I didn't like the judgment it implied, especially a judgment from ignorance.

Nonetheless, there is an implied judgment in both offering forgiveness and receiving it. To accept forgiveness is to accept judgment. And that was the beautiful thing about this paralytic. He was willing to accept the fact that he was a sinner.

We do not hear him protesting to his four friends that he is not a sinner. We do not hear him cursing God as he is lowered down through the roof, shouting, "What did I do to deserve this?" Or "Why did this have to happen to me?" Instead, he seems to have answered as Katherine Hepburn answered recently, "Why shouldn't it happen to me?" The paralytic was humble enough to accept the fact that he was a sinner. Consequently, he was also humble enough to experience real forgiveness and healing.

Theologian Paul Tillich likes to point out that "understanding does not replace judging."[1] Says Tillich, "Our immensely increased insight into the conditions of human existence should not undercut our courage to call wrong."[2] Brought into our own time, we Christians need to reaffirm wrong as wrong.

In the present threat of an AIDS epidemic to accompany the already existing epidemic of herpes and other sex-related diseases, we need to say again that fornication, promiscuity and adultery are wrong. We can understand why they happen, but understanding and approving and declaring them as normative Christian behavior is unfaithful to what Jesus and Paul and others have said.

Comedian Steve Epstein notes: "To appease God, Oral Roberts accepted $1.3 million from a guy who owns a race track. I guess this means gambling could never be a sin. Too bad Jim Bakker didn't send the $1.3 million — then maybe God would loosen up on adultery."

But God hasn't loosened up on adultery. Healing and forgiveness can come when we are willing to accept judgment. If judgment has come to Jim Bakker, then so should forgiveness and healing. God forgives ministers too!

But healing and forgiveness do come when we accept judgment. Psychoanalysts, counselors, ministers and psychiatrists know that. We resent being judged by anyone, even God, so counselors hope they will be able to lead us to the point where we recognize the unconscious judgment we have already made of ourselves and the unconscious guilt we have thus imposed. Thus the guilt becomes a burden and the fear of really being found out paralyzes us.

But when we come to the truth about ourselves, when we come clean with our consciences without rationalization and self-justification, when we allow the penetrating insight to cut deeply and to judge us, we can also then sense the power of forgiveness.

———

People with the power to forgive also recognize that forgiveness is a gift, not an achievement.

Nearly all religions and all belief systems fall into the trap of legalism — Christianity included. Most all of us think we must somehow earn forgiveness or deserve it. Paul Tillich astutely observes that forgiveness "is too great as a gift and too humiliating as a judgment. We want to contribute something, and if we have learned that we cannot contribute anything positive, then we try at least to contribute something negative: the pain of self-accusation and self-rejection."[3]

Many of us self-sufficient types do have difficulty accepting gifts. On the one hand we feel we do not deserve them, but on the other hand we feel we deserve more. But more than that, we rightly feel acceptance of the gift implies obligation, that we then "owe them one." Consequently, even our gift giving degenerates into a legalistic point system of who owes what to whom.

Thus to receive a gift is an affront to our pride. To receive forgiveness as a gift is even more humiliating; but it is precisely the humility we need to be healed, to be liberated from all the odious self-righteousness that separates us from one another and from God.

The big breakthrough with Saul, the zealous Pharisee, came when we saw how obnoxious all his super-religiosity was, not only to his fellow man, but to God. Taking great pride in his pedigree, his productivity and his astonishing achievements, Saul had attempted to storm heaven, as it were, to demand God give him a place of honor.

But then the breakthrough came, the penetrating, life-changing insight, that he really was an arrogant, self-righteous, obnoxious braggart. All the things he had counted as important he now saw as so much dung compared to God's free gift of grace and forgiveness lavished upon him through Jesus Christ. And the religion that had become so defensive, so legalistic, so burdensome and irksome, now became a delight. He was accepted, included, forgiven, not on the basis of his meritorious law-keeping, but on the basis of God's gracious judgment which intends not to destroy, but to heal and make whole.

The forgiven person experiences God not so much as judge, but as lover. But religiosity wants always to make God the lawyer who demands perfect obedience before he will love and forgive. Not so, says Jesus. God is ready to forgive those ready to accept his forgiveness as a gift. That is why the paralytic was healed and why the theological fact-finding team from Jerusalem was so angry. They wanted to make God's love and forgiveness conditional. They wanted it to be a reward for law keeping and achievement. To offer forgiveness to anyone who was humble enough to accept it was an affront to their pride and legalism.

If then we are to experience self-acceptance, if we are to experience liberation and healing, if we are to know true grace and renewal, we shall have to have the humility to accept the forgiveness as a gift of God.

However, *people with power to forgive will need to give and receive forgiveness from each other.*

Once when talking with a wedding couple I said some of the most important words for a healthy marriage are "I am sorry. I was wrong. Please forgive me." One bride responded she could readily say, "I am sorry," and "Please forgive me." But she found it almost impossible to say, "I was wrong."

Most of us have the same problem. We have immense difficulty admitting we were wrong. Oh, to be sure, we readily see where the other is wrong. We are quick to point out the faults of the other guy. We are glad to excuse and rationalize our own faults, but we usually are not so charitable with the other fellow. What are major crimes in the other fellow are only misdemeanors when we do them.

When we are honest we know the truth of Jesus' saying that we should remove the wooden beam from our own eye before we try to remove the speck of sawdust from our brother's eye. The judgment by which we judge does have a way of coming back to judge us. The Word of God is always a two-edged sword, penetrating not only the person to whom it is directed, but also the handler. (How well we ministers know that.)

The word "forgive" literally means to give the life back again to start over again, to start over anew and afresh. Yet, in our grudge-bearing this is precisely what we fail to do. A grudge is a claim on another person's life. That person has done us wrong — either a real or a perceived wrong — and we will not let him forget it. We do not let him forget it because the grudge gives us power over him. We "have something" on him. We can inhibit his life and hold it over him. We can quietly await our chance to get even, to take our revenge. We can make him live in fear, never knowing when we will ambush him psychologically. Consequently, we make life like the armed battlefield that it is.

But there is an ironic twist to grudge-bearing. Bearing the grudge becomes a life-draining burden. While we are waiting to get even, to right the wrong, the world is out dancing. Grudge-bearing is something like carrying around radioactive nuclear waste, ready to hurl it at our enemy, only to find that the radioactivity is destroying us.

And think of the radioactivity destroying so many marriages, so many families, so many relationships. We are offended, we get angry, we carry a grudge and won't let it go until we get our pound of flesh. Grudge bearers are self-righteous and cannot forgive because they have not been forgiven and cannot forgive themselves.

Is forgiveness real? Is it possible? Yes, says Jesus to the legalistic, fact-finding theologians from Jerusalem, forgiveness is real and possible because God is love and always has been. God is not a legalist. God is a lover, says Jesus, and he created people to be lovers, to be forgivers, to practice and to experience the power of forgiveness.

Not only does God have power to forgive, so does the Son of Man and the sons and daughters of men, the new humanity. In fact, Jesus even goes so far to say that if we expect forgiveness from God, we ought to forgive one another. "Forgive us our trespasses as we forgive those who tresspass against us," Christendom prays each week. We have the power within us to give up the grudge, to lay aside the tired, old claims, to forgive and forget the wrongs done to us, especially if we are honest enough to see the wrongs we have done to others.

In the movie, *The Mission*, one of the leading characters is converted from being a slave-trader of Brazilian Indians to be a Jesuit priest. But he insists on doing penance, dragging a heavy bundle through the jungle back to the Indians he used to enslave. Once back, in a dramatic, cliff-side scene, where the bundle threatened to make him fall, the Indians cut away the bundle. The people he had formerly enslaved forgave him and set him free. We have the power to do that for each other.

As Martin Luther pointed out centuries ago, we are a priesthood of believers who are to be priests for one another, forgiving one another as God for Christ's sake has forgiven us. We do have the power to forgive as God's sons and daughters. Or as Jesus said even centuries earlier, "Receive the Holy Spirit. If you forgive the sins of any, they are forgiven; if you retain the sins of any, they are retained."

We have received the Holy Spirit. Let us therefore be people who exercise our power to forgive.

---

1. Tillich, Paul. *The New Being,* (New York: Charles Scribner's Sons, 1955), p. 5.

2. *Ibid.*

3. *Op.cit.,* p. 8.

The Holy Trinity
John 16:12-15

The Divine Advocacy

The season following Pentecost often coincides with Memorial Day and it tends to be overshadowed by parades and visits to cemeteries and memories of those loved long since and lost a while. Even more than that, it is overshadowed by the official opening of summer for those of us in northern states. Memorial weekend is for opening cottages, launching boats and for getting a good start on a summer tan.

But the Festival of Pentecost has been around about 19 centuries longer than Memorial Day (which was begun in 1868) and no doubt will be observed long after Memorial Day is itself dead and forgotten.

Pentecost means 50, and refers to the 50th day following Easter. According to the Gospels and Book of Acts, for 40 days the resurrected Jesus appeared to his disciples and then ascended into heaven. But on the Jewish festival day of Pentecost, 50 days after Easter, we are told the Holy Spirit of God came upon the disciples in the city of Jerusalem.

Unusual phenomena accompanied this occurrence. There was the sound of a mighty rushing wind. Strange phenomena which appeared to be tongues of fire rested upon the disciples' heads. And they were given the ability to understand one another even though they spoke a variety of languages.

Peter and the apostles said that this event was in fulfillment of the prophecies of Joel, the prophet, who said that in the latter days God would pour out his Spirit upon his people. Moreover, it was also the fulfillment of the promise of Jesus that after he departed from them, he would send his Spirit to them to be their helper or advocate.

As a result of the coming of the Holy Spirit of God on Pentecost, the Christian church was brought into being. It was the early part of June, about 30 A.D., in the city of Jerusalem. Peter was inspired to preach the first Gospel sermon about the divine significance of Jesus' death and resurrection. This one whom a sinful age had crucified, God had made both Lord and Christ by his resurrection from the dead.

Now, said Peter, God was beginning a new humanity with Jesus Christ at the head. If the first Adam had disobeyed God to be subject to the powers of death, Jesus had obeyed God to become subject to the powers of life eternal. Thus the coming of his Spirit is the assurance that God has not given up on humankind. Instead, by his Spirit, he intends to be man's advocate, his counselor and helper.

This was in keeping with what Jesus earlier had told them, as recorded by John's gospel. Physically, he was going away. But their movement would not be stopped by his death. Instead, by his resurrected and living Spirit, he would convict the world of sin and lead them into all truth. Just as the Incarnation had been evidence of God's forbearing love for the world, so would the coming of the Spirit be a sign of God's continuing advocacy for the development of our full humanity under the headship of Christ. God was not giving up on mankind. Instead, by his Spirit, he would continue to manifest his presence and power in the world to convict of sin and to lead into truth.

Therefore, on this Pentecost Sunday, this birthday of the Christian Church, we celebrate two aspects of the divine advocacy — the conviction of sin and the leading into all truth.

Consider the Spirit's power to convict of sin.
In his Pentecost sermon, Peter was intent to show how wrong the rulers in Jerusalem had been in convicting and crucifying Jesus. Both political and religious leaders had conspired to put Jesus to death because he was an unsettling challenge to their basis of power. They had determined that reality was to be defined by cynical religion and the politics of brute power.

Among other things, the contest at the cross had to do with definitions of ultimate reality and authority. Jesus bet his life on sincere obedience to God and the eschewing of violence. He laid his life on the line for the cause of righteousness, justice and truth. And although the crucifixion appeared to be a defeat, the resurrection, said Peter, was God's vindication of Jesus. The principalities and powers were wrong and Jesus was right. And by his resurrection and Spirit, God was convicting the world of sin.

And the Spirit still is convicting the principalities and powers of sin. It was the confessing Christians of Germany who stood up against Naziism and all its atrocities. If Jesus stood against the holocaust theology learned from the Old Testament where "pure religion" was thought best protected by eliminating "impure people," Christians of conscience have called for resistance to the brutal and blatant holocaust powers. Rather than obliterate a total people with all their children and cattle as part of the Old Testament and Naziism taught, Jesus advocated willing the good for the enemy and conversion by gentle persuasion and the sincere witness of the life of faith.

Or consider the witness of the Spirit with respect to Ethiopia, Somalia and other starving countries. The conscience of the Christian world was moved to raise millions of dollars to send millions of tons of food to these countries. The outpouring of love and compassion has indeed been overwhelming.

However, the Marxist Ethiopian government, headed by Colonel Mengista, charged exorbitant port entry fees to the very ships delivering millions of tons of free foodstuffs to his starving peoples. Not only did he profiteer off the Christian heart of compassion, he blocked shipment of free food to his dying people, especially those in the rebel territories of Eritrea. Let us be assured of this, the living Spirit of Christ works to convict corrupt and inhuman government. The principalities and powers will not prevail forever.

However, the Spirit of God exposes sin not only in society and the corrupt systems of government. It penetrates to the innermost reaches of our own hearts to expose the evil and to bring the self to the divine light. It is by the gentle nudging of Christ's Spirit that we are saved from the suffocation of obsessive materialism and the exhaustion of compulsive achieving.

Many Americans are so caught up in the obsession with success at any cost that they want to make their mark, even if it is only as brief as a Roman candle on the Fourth of July. Many Americans are typified by drama critic Walter Kerr's friend who said that he was afraid that if he did not hurry up he would not achieve his goals before he had his heart attack, but that if he did not slow down, he was going to have his heart attack before he achieved his goals.

The living Spirit of Christ reminded us of the sin of presumption wherein we think we must build a paradise of our own, rather than receive it as a gift from God. The Spirit of the humble, self-sacrificing Christ convicts us of our pride wherein we must declare our self-worth in God's eyes by overwhelming achievement and success. It is this Spirit which stands over against brazen, selfish sensuality. It is this Spirit which witnesses to our worth as total human beings, rather than just as sex objects controlled by eros. It is this Spirit which releases us from the grip of hedonism and the suffocation of narcissism.

As on Pentecost, so today, the Spirit of God continues to bring judgment upon the world in its corruption. And it judges us in our inward corruption, to save us from destruction and death.

Consider also the *Spirit's power to lead into all truth.*

On the day of Pentecost Peter preached to the assembled thousands convincing them of the truth of Jesus' life. The authorities had declared Jesus an imposter, liar, traitor, disturber of the peace and blasphemer, and thereby had him put to death. But God raised him from the dead to prove God true and every man a liar, says Paul. And said Peter and the Gospel of John, Christ is indeed God's way and truth and life.

Well-known biblical scholar and translator, J. B. Phillips, has lamented that many Christians today are living on the spiritual capital of the past — a spiritual capital that is rapidly being depleted. Says the Rev. Dr. Phillips, "Our society ... bears all the marks of a God-starved community. There is little real moral authority because no ultimate Authority is known or acknowledged."[1] As a result, says Dr. Phillips, many see little purpose in life. "Most ... hold on, without much reason or authority to the moral standards of what is commonly supposed to be the good life."[2] Consequently, many of us become locked into a comfortable materialism and cozy agnosticism.

But that is not the way of the Spirit. It is the advocate of truth, willing to do its work with men and women open to it. Consider some of the martyrs of Christian history who risked themselves for the truth for our great benefit.

What power the message of the Bible has had for truth. And how men have violently resisted it in the past to protect their vested interests as today they resist it in totalitarian countries. But our resistance is not violent, but passive. We do not hate the Bible, we ignore it. We do not wish its extinction except by default through neglect. It has for centuries been the agent of the Spirit, but says J. B. Phillips, we really have not studied it with an adult mind. Note how hard it is to get people to study the Bible in an adult way.

If Pastor John Robinson assured the Pilgrims there was yet more light to break from God's blessed word of truth, so would Jesus assure his eternal flock of pilgrims that it is God's desire to liberate us from closed systems of thought. If we are bored, if we find life tiresome, if we are overwhelmed with skepticism and pessimism, is it not time for us to open ourselves again to the Spirit of Truth?

The greatest scientists are the humblest scientists. They are overwhelmed by how little they know and how great the mysteries yet to be discovered. So too in the life of faith and thought. It is the childish mind which suffers from arrested development. But it is the childlike mind that is ever open to new truth. Agnosticism can become as much a prison as ignorance.

The Spirit would awaken us to the truth that God is not a distant, unknowable mystery, totally unconcerned with the world. Rather, as Phillips says, God has focused himself in Jesus Christ, to manifest his being in a man, to show for certain that God's attitude toward mankind is one of unremitting love. By the Incarnation, the "enfleshment," God has demonstrated his advocacy for the world of man. It is, says Dorothy Sayers, "God taking his own medicine," entering into humanity to advocate for its coming to the truth and love of God.

We pray to be open to the Spirit of God so as to be convicted of the sin which destroys us and to be led into the truth which would make us whole. The Spirit, the great liberator of thought, would teach us more and more, knowing the more we know, the more we are able to know.

And the Spirit would teach us we are not living in a lunatic and chaotic world, but in a part of a law-abiding universe, the greatest law of which is love, as demonstrated in the death and resurrection of Jesus. And the challenge is this: should it be true that we admit that this earth has been visited by the Creator, if God has focused himself in the Christ, then the values and standards of this Son of God will inevitably challenge and judge our lives. But by the same token, for those open and humble, this same Spirit wishes not to judge to destroy, but to convict to bring us to the truth to make us whole.

For as John's gospel says, "God so loved the world that he gave his only Son, that whoever believes on Him should not perish but have everlasting life. For God sent not his Son into the world to condemn the world, but to save it and make it whole" (John 3:16-17).

This is the Divine Advocacy.

---

1. Phillips, J. B. *God, Our Contemporary,* (New York: Macmillan, 1960), p. VIII.

2. *Ibid.,* p. 6.

Corpus Christi
Luke 9:11-17

Five Thousand For Lunch In Galilee

My friend remembers it well. It was Advent season and he and his wife had decided to invite all their church board members and their spouses to their home for an Advent Supper.

The invitations went out and 110 responded! Gathering in their home in a festive mood, people were everywhere. After the Doxology and Grace, my friend's wife served the multitude with her usual aplomb. People were sitting on the stairs and chairs, on floors and footstools, and standing in corners and hallways. The had 110 for Advent Supper. It was the *first* time they had ever had that many for a meal. And, it was the *last* time!

Since that occasion, said his wife, they have entertained many people in their home — sometimes as many as 60 for dinner, but never again 110. They like to entertain. Or better said, they like to be together with people enjoying good food and drink. Sharing food and conversations with one another can be sacramental occasions — occasions of knowing and being known, times when friendships are firmly formed.

Jesus also enjoyed being with people around table with good food and drink — so much so he was accused of being a glutton and winebibber. He seems to have been invited out to dinner more than he entertained in his own home in

Capernaum. But on those occasions when he does host a meal, the food seems to become almost sacramental as in the last supper and the dinner at Emmaus and in the breakfast on the beach.

In Luke chapter 9 we have another occasion where Jesus is host for lunch. My friends were hosts for 110, but Jesus is now host for 5,000 for lunch, and that's just the men, not counting the women and children. Besides he was out in the hills of Galilee far away from sources of food. It would take a miracle to feed 5,000 for lunch anywhere, let alone in the wilderness.

In response to Jesus' request for food, John's gospel says that Phillip the pessimist said it would take $40 to $50 worth of bread to feed the multitude even if he could find a place to buy it. Enterprising Andrew, with only a glimmer of hope, said, "There's a boy here with five barley loaves and two fish — but what are they among so many?"

Jesus asked them to sit down in groups of 50, and then taking the loaves and fish, he gave thanks and began to distribute the food. When it was all over, the crowd of 5,000 men plus women and children which supposedly had no food for lunch in the wilderness now had 12 baskets full of leftovers, one for each of the 12 apostles. The truths of God were once again made known in a kind of sacramental meal for 5,000 in Galilee.

One truth learned at lunch in Galilee is that *when we share there is usually more than enough for everyone.*

What happened that day at lunch? Did Jesus miraculously multiply the bread and fish, so that there was enough for everyone? If at Cana of Galilee he changed water into wine, on the slopes around the Sea of Galilee, could he not have stretched five loaves into 5,000? Of course. That may well be what happened.

But let me suggest an alternative interpretation. John's gospel tells us it was Passover season. That means thousands of pilgrims would have been on their way to Jerusalem. Most likely many in Jesus' crowd had provisions for the journey. But when it came time for lunch, they were afraid to take out their food, fearing the thousands without food would stare at them or even take it away. Or at best, they were too polite to eat in the presence of people without food.

The innocent boy had not been so coy as to hide his food. It was plainly visible. And with an innocent and generous heart he offered to share. Using this act of generosity Jesus gave thanks and began to distribute the bread. He knew people had food if only they would be willing to share. The boy's innocence and generosity and Jesus' public acts and prayers were the catalyst for a wonderful lunch for 5,000 in Galilee.

We are reminded of the familiar children's story about stone soup. Two poor travelers came into a European village and asked for food, but the suspicious villagers refused, claiming they hardly had enough for themselves. The travelers cleverly offered to make stone soup for everyone. The reluctant villagers agreed. As the stones cooked in the water they suggested potatoes would improve the soup and so some villagers brought potatoes. The travelers then suggested onions, tomatoes and other vegetables would help, so the villagers brought those. On and on, it continued until they were sitting down to a sumptuous feast for all. The food was there. All they had to do was share.

When Paul advised the Corinthian and Galatian Christians to sow the seed of the Spirit, he was urging them to take a chance on sharing what they had been given. His legalistic critics claimed the bread of life was only for those who kept their religious laws in their way. They tended to be restrictive, defensive and exclusive.

But Paul enjoins us to sow to the Spirit. We are to see God as leading us into the life of productivity and prosperity instead of calling us back into defensiveness and fear. Legalism and narrow religion tend to be past-oriented, confining us to the peak experience of past generations, rehearsing their insights, visions, and victories without launching out to experience what God has for us in our own time. And this is as true in the material life as it is in the spiritual.

A fundamental truth of nature and of God often has been forgotten. Nature and God grow exponentially, geometrically, rather than by simple addition. We can count the seeds in an apple, but who can count the apples in a single seed which grows into a tree to produce apples and seeds for years to come? We are advised to take the risk of sowing to the Spirit — that is, seeing God as living and active, seeing God as merciful and compassionate, desiring that all people share in the riches of his grace both materially and spiritually.

In his book, *Wealth And Poverty*, George Gilder says, "It is the idea of economic futility — not capitalistic growth — that gives license to the culture of hedonism and sensuality."[1] It is the loss of hope, the succumbing to despair, that creates a people resigned to eating, drinking, and being merry for tomorrow they die.

Philosopher Charles Pierce has said that faith, hope and love "are the gifts that work together to free mankind from the bondage of power and the dead hand of the past and open us to the possibilities of the divine."[2] Any religion which constricts God's expansiveness is doomed to spiritual starvation. And any church which continues to constrict, to control excessively, to thwart adventure, to stifle risk, and crush creativity is bound to stagnate. The principle of God and nature is to get the seed out of the granary and to sow it in spite of the risk of failure. We are to share the five loaves and two fishes we have. This will provide great spiritual and material excitement for a new future for all.

Most everyone believes we ought to share out of our abundance. But now comes the tough one. Jesus also teaches *we are to share out of our poverty,* like the poor boy who gave his five loaves and two fish.

We do not often speak of the miserly heart of the poor. It is not often said, but it is nevertheless true, that the poor can be as greedy, as selfish, as in love with money as the rich. Greed is no respecter of persons. A church I know has a clothes closet where it gives away used clothing free to the poor who need it. But one poor woman comes in regularly, scoops up as much as she can carry for free, and then goes and sells the clothing to the very poor the church is trying to help.

How different the attitude of the poor widow of Jesus' story who gave everything she had, her last two coins, to share in the cause of God. She gave with a reckless generosity, with an openness and trust that has been an example to the world ever since. The lines of the poet describe her: "An incidental greatness charactered her unconsidered ways ...." She is a reminder of how God often uses insignificant people of faith and love to turn the tide of history and to remind us that the world was made for love and sharing and risk-taking.

The cynical realist might well say that temples and churches cannot be run on widow's mites, and they are right. But what they fail to see is that churches could run very well on the widow's generosity. She had the generosity, but not the money; whereas many of us often have the money but not the generosity. Consequently, she was the key to the future, the example of the noble, generous, sharing life of the coming kingdom.

But let us remember she is an example not only for the rich, but also for the poor. Very often the poor attempt to excuse themselves from sharing and loving, but there is no such excuse in the Bible. God can bless the gifts of the poor as well as the rich. The disciples found the small boy with five barley loaves and a couple of fish; "But what is that among so many," they said to Jesus. But the boy, poor as he was, was willing to share, and with Jesus' blessing, the hearts of all were opened to share so that all were fed with plenty left over.

Recall Jesus' story of the talents where three people were given five, three and one talents, respectively. Many of us, like the parable, are one talent people. So we hold it back, keep it to ourselves, bury it, or hoard it like a miser, asking, "What is that among so many?" We have difficulty believing our small gift or task or talent will make any difference. But with the blessing of Christ, it multiplies its effectiveness.

Very often it is the small gift that blesses the world. A doctor recently wrote a letter of thanks to a teacher who had challenged him and encouraged him 30 years earlier. The following week he received a reply written in a shaky hand which said: "My dear Willie: I want you to know what your note meant to me. I am an old lady in my 80s, living alone in a small room, cooking my own meals, lonely, and seeming like the last leaf on the tree. You will be interested to know, Willie, that I taught school for 50 years and in all that time, yours is the first letter of appreciation I have ever received. It came on a cold, blue morning and cheered my lonely old heart as nothing has cheered me in many years." In this case the doctor gave the widow's mite.

The widow's mite is often mighty in its power of love and sharing. Many churches are blessed by widows of modest means who give a far greater percentage of their income and time than people of more ample means. And on the larger scale, it is well known that churches of the poorer classes of people give much more per capita than churches of the wealthier classes of people. Nevertheless, the poor might say as Peter and John said to the cripple at the Beautiful Gate of the Temple: "Silver and gold have I none, but such as I have, I give unto thee." Greed is no more excusable among the poor than among the rich. Everyone, no matter how poor, has something to share.

Of course, sometimes people are not always ready for what we want to share. Newscaster Walter Cronkite and his wife, Betsy, were going to entertain a popular artist who was also a well-known gourmet. The Cronkites worried about what to serve such an educated palate. "Let's serve him family style," said Cronkite. So Mrs. Cronkite, a good Southern cook, decided to serve her favorite fried chicken, black-eyed peas, and cornbread.

The night came and the artist-gourmet arrived at the Cronkites' New York apartment. The artist laid his sable across a chair and exclaimed, "Thank God. It's so good to be back in civilization. I've just returned from three awful weeks in the deep South, where all they serve is fried chicken, black-eyed peas and cornbread." We do have to exercise prudence as we share.

For both poor and rich, giving often comes long after all our priorities of gaining and getting. We always want more, but we have to ask, how much more is enough? Greed so often overshadows gratitude, and compulsive acquisitiveness so frequently overrides thankfulness. But as Paul Scherer likes to say, love is a spendthrift and leaves its arithmetic at home. Love is always in the red and God is love.

Let no one be deceived. The widow's mite is not to be a way for monied matrons to buy off their consciences for a few paltry pennies. Nor are the five loaves and two fish meant to limit our generosity. Rather, they are to be examples of adventurous faith and generous love for both poor and rich.

---

1. Gilder, George. *Wealth And Poverty,* (New York: Basic Books, Inc., 1981), p. 260.

2. *Ibid.,* p. 267.

Ordinary Time 9
Luke 7:1-10

Finding Faith
In Unlikely People

One of the continuing delights of life is the joy of the unexpected. Highly scheduled as we are, and rigorously regimented, occasionally we are extraordinarily pleased with interruption and variation. When out-of-town friends turn up unannounced, rather than having scheduled themselves weeks in advance, we experience a certain excitement. How pleasant to have a business deal grow into undreamed proportions. What joy in having a surprise verdict from judge and jury. What a thrill to see surgery and medication do far more than expected. Thankfully, life has innumerable surprises.

Our text centers on Jesus' surprise at finding faith in an unlikely person. He expected his fellow Israelites to be responsive to his word. They shared with him a common heritage and faith, a regularized way of seeing and thinking.

But a Roman Centurion was something else! Who would expect to find a sincere faith in him? He was a man of authority and power. Not only was he an outsider, he represented the hated enemy. A man of talent and intelligence, the Centurion of Capernaum, believed nevertheless. And Jesus could not contain his delight at this unexpected discovery of faith in an unlikely person. "I tell you," he said, "nowhere, even in Israel, have I found faith like this."

Like Jesus, *one unlikely place we find faith is in people of authority and power* — unlikely because we assume power and faith are mutually exclusive. The more powerful you are the less you need faith — or so we sometimes say.

Notice on the one hand this view holds religion to be mainly a crutch for the weak and cowardly. It serves as a kind of divine apron string behind which we can safely view the ordeals of the world. It sees faith as a sop for the superstitious, a hiding place for the timid.

One problem with this view is the fallacious presumption man needs no outside help, that he can, if he will, stand on his own two feet without psychological crutches and canes. But where do you find a man like that, one who lives without support of any kind? In the '60s it was popular to write of man come-of-age, the secular man, a sort of deified playboy, sophisticated, cool, worldly-wise, self-contained, self-sufficient, reserved, independent, a connoisseur of wines and women, a distinguished man among men who had his head together, who was never fooled or taken. This '60s man come-of-age never sinned, though he might have made errors in judgment because he didn't have all the facts. Consequently, he claimed no guilt, was oblivious to remorse and regret, and viewed the world as the survival of the fittest. Most assuredly, he was fit, and he was surviving.

Or was he really? Carrying some of these attitudes into the use of power wreaked havoc to careers and reputations, and assaulted with cool contempt the institutions and principles which give this nation some of its uniqueness. Tough, cool, calculating, our man-at-the-top, embodying for many the ideal man-come-of-age, believed power was the whole name of the game. Power. Period. Nothing more. Get before you are gotten, strike before you are stricken, push before you are pushed, destroy before you are destroyed. It's one thing to make mistakes; it's quite another to sin against the foundations of a democracy. The so-called modern secular man doesn't need a crutch, doesn't need anything to hold him up. But irony of ironies, every Achilles has a vulnerable heel.

Or consider another manifestation of the power and authority mentality — money. Not long ago, I had the pleasure of hearing a well-known independent press correspondent. He gave interesting insights into the world situation. Money is the name of the game, he said. All international disputes are reducible to money.

But is that really true? Of course money is important. Of course economic matters play a huge role in world peace. Undoubtedly wars are fought over money, and its power. But to reduce everything to money-making is distortion and oversimplification. He said as much when he went on to relate a most interesting incident in the Mid-East. Syria, at that time considerably anti-American and pro-Russian, finally came to the point where they wanted to negotiate with Israel. Who did Syria want to arbitrate the discussions? Russia? No, America! Why? Because, he said, they knew America would be fair and compassionate.

Well, then, so power and money are not the whole name of the game in international relations. Fairness and compassion enter in. Brutality is counterbalanced with gentleness and consideration for the other point of view. He went on to say Americans are respected around the world because they help the weak, feed the hungry, clothe the naked, heal the sick. Power isn't the whole name of the game. Rather, it is the conviction that human life is sacred, even human life that is weak or faltering, in need of someone to lean on.

Note another aspect of power and authority. The Centurion who came to Jesus, not only was willing to confess his need of help, he also recognized the derivative sources of power. In other words, he knew ultimately power and authority came from outside himself. He recognized himself as a channel, a distributor of power.

He saw Jesus in a similar role. The Centurion commanded soldiers in the name of Caesar; Jesus commanded evil spirits in the name of God. Both saw themselves as channels of higher power and authority. As Jesus said, "I can do nothing on my own authority ... because I seek not my own will but the will of him who sent me" (John 5:30). At his trial Pilate derided Jesus saying, "You will not speak to me? Do you not know that I have power to release you, and power to crucify you?" Jesus answered him, "You would have no power over me unless it had been given you from above ..." (John 19:10-11). Pilate believed his power came from Caesar. Jesus believed Caesar's power came from God, as did his own. All power is derivative, and finally it is derived from God.

Government cynics see America's power as derived from missiles, planes, guns, aircraft carriers, the Pentagon and institutions of government. Actually, America's strength is derived from the consent of the governed, and the consent of the governed is founded upon principles and ideals which have divine origins. Ultimately, America's power is derived from God. Consequently, its power will fade proportionally to its loss of faith in God and concern for Godly principles.

Cynics see legal power as derived from lawmakers, lawyers, and the judiciary. But all laws rest squarely on the will of the people, and the will of the people rests on principles, values and ideals which are divine in origin. Ultimately, man's law rests upon the law of God. Likewise medicine rests upon the power of healing which comes from God. All power is derivative power.

The temptation of man is to believe he has done it all by himself, that he is sufficient unto himself, that he has originated his own power. That is why Jesus was delighted to see a man of authority have such depth of understanding. He found faith in God in an unlikely person. Does he find it in us?

Jesus was also surprised to find faith in the Centurion because he was an outsider and an enemy. He expected his insider friends to have faith, but not his outsider enemy.

One of the persistent surprises in Biblical history is God's use of the outsider. Joseph was thrown out by his brothers and sold into slavery, but God brought him in again to change history. In Egypt, the Hebrews were outsiders and slaves, but

God freed them up and gave them their own land. Moses was meek, and poor at making speeches, yet God used him as the leader. David was the youngest and unlikeliest of Jesse's sons, yet God made him king. Amos was neither a prophet nor the son of a prophet, yet his message became God's message. Cyrus, the non-Jew, the conquering Persian king, is called God's Messiah by Isaiah. Jesus himself was scorned as an outsider Northerner by the elitist Southern circle of pretenders to the throne. "Can anything good come out of Nazareth?" (of the North) they asked sneeringly.

Drawing on the universalism of some of the great prophets, Jesus taught that God was not the exclusive possession of the chosen people. He knew what Isaiah meant when he said:

> *See, they come; some from far away,*
> *These from the north and those from the west*
>   *and these from the land of Syene. (Isaiah 49:12)*

He was acquainted with Malachi's prophecy:

> *From furthest east to furthest west my*
> *name is great among the nations. (Malachi 1:11)*

While Jesus may have begun his ministry with a rather exclusivistic view of God as Israel's sole possession, he soon expanded his vision to behold the amazing work of God throughout the world, even in the Romans, the enemies. What a breakthrough. Heretofore, with the exception of some of the prophets, God was seen as a national deity. The Jews were not alone in this belief. Most nations had their special god or gods. He was theirs exclusively, and devoted his divine powers to gaining victories and prosperity for them.

Very often America has had the too-easy assumption that God is on our side, that he always will give us victory and prosperity because we stand for righteousness, truth, and morality. Freedom is God's aim for man, and since America extols and celebrates freedom, God will always spare her, or so we sometimes think.

But consider the scandals, the fraud, the embezzlements, the sexual abuse and harassment charges laid at the feet of many of our national business leaders and politicians. Each day the newspapers report some new violation, some new breach of public trust, some new crime fueled by greed and the lust for power. Sometimes leaders in our so-called "enemy" nations and businesses demonstrate a higher morality than our own.

Consider another public leader, the Rev. Dr. Henry Pitney Van Dusen, 77, and his wife, Elizabeth, 80. Dr. Van Dusen, an ecumenical Presbyterian, headed Union Theological Seminary of New York, and brought it to its pinnacle of influence with such notables as Paul Tillich and Reinhold Niebuhr on the faculty. In recent years Dr. Van Dusen lost his speech due to a stroke and Mrs. Van Dusen suffered severely from arthritis. Consequently, a few years ago, in their Princeton, New Jersey, home they wrote a suicide note, and then ended their lives with a massive dose of sleeping pills. The note alluded to their failing health, their inability to do what they wanted to do, and their faith in a life after death. The note ended with the prayer: "O Lamb of God, that takest away the sins of the world, have mercy upon us. O Lamb of God, that takest away the sins of the world, grant us thy peace."

It was not passive euthanasia. It wasn't a matter of pulling the plug. It was *active* euthanasia, entered into with a sound mind. While I do not know the intensity of pain, the emptiness and loneliness, the sense of worthlessness which the Van Dusens suffered, and while I would not be quick to pass judgment, I would raise some questions and observations.

It is fair to say that many Christians over the centuries have suffered worse than the Van Dusens. Some have undergone extreme torture for their faith. Others have endured unbelievable hardships. Still others have suffered loneliness, deprivation, poverty, despair, deep doubt. Nevertheless they endured. Dietrich Bonhoeffer, German theologian arrested, imprisoned, and eventually executed by Hitler, said years ago: "God has reserved to himself the right to determine the end of life, because he alone knows the goal to which it is His will to lead it. Even if (a person's) earthly life has become a torment for him, he must commit it intact to God's hand, from which it came."[1]

The Van Dusens were insiders, leaders at the very heart of world Christianity. By contrast, consider another Christian, a woman alone, frail, weak, sickly: an outsider, unknown in important Christian circles. Yet she found her purpose and life-work in prayer from her wheelchair. Every day she prayed for the church, the ministers, those in need. She was so weak in body, she hardly could speak. Nevertheless, when God adds it all up, he may count the work of prayer during her feeblest years as the most significant work of all. Like Jesus, we find deep faith and unselfishness in unlikely people.

As Jesus observed long ago, "Many, I tell you, will come from east and west to feast with Abraham, Isaac and Jacob in the Kingdom of Heaven. But those who were born to the Kingdom will be driven out into the dark, the place of wailing and grinding of teeth" (Matthew 8:11-12). It is not a matter of being an insider, said Jesus, not a matter of ecclesiastical aristocracy or religious pedigree, but a matter of faith — faith which is open and possible for all.

Notice further that *Jesus was surprised with the Centurion's faith in his word.* The Centurion may have had some opportunity to be exposed to the wisdom of Rome and Greece. Undoubtedly he was intelligent and capable. Yet he was teachable, ready to believe what Jesus had to say.

Very often today, the assumption is that the more intelligent you are and the more you know, the less faith you need. Faith often is regarded as the instrumentality of the credulous and feebleminded. But for those who are truly enlightened, those really in-the-know, faith is superfluous, or so the argument sometimes goes. Knowing this, Jesus was delighted to find faith in a man who might have regarded himself as intellectually sophisticated.

One of the sins of Jesus' contemporaries was the belief they had it all in the bag, that God had given them his complete revelation and knowledge of himself. But it was that very belief that closed them off to the new that was happening in their midst. "Woe to you, Chorazin! Woe to you, Bethsaida! for if the mighty works done in you had been done in Tyre and Sidon, they would have repented long ago in sack cloth and ashes.... And you, Capernaum, will you be exalted to heaven? You shall be brought down to Hades. For if the mighty works done in you had been done in Sodom, it would have remained until this day. But I tell you that it shall be more tolerable on the day of judgment for the land of Sodom than for you" (Matthew 11:21-24).

The outsiders were more receptive to the truth than the insiders. Consequently Jesus prayed, "I thank thee, Father, Lord of heaven and earth, that thou hast hidden these things from the wise and understanding and revealed them to babes; yea Father, for such was thy gracious will" (Matthew 11:25-26). A childlike openness is necessary to receive new truth. Very often our sophisticated intellectualisms prevent us from seeing the new truth trying to break in upon us. Regrettably, education sometimes causes us to be arrogant and blasé, whereas, it should awaken humility and wonder.

As Elizabeth Barrett Browning wrote:

> *Earth's crammed with heaven*
> *And every bush a flame with God.*
> *But only he who sees takes off his shoes.*
> *The rest sit round it, and pluck blackberries*
> *And daub their natural faces unaware ....*

As New Testament scholars Major, Manson and Wright have written, "The window lets in the light, but not to the blind. It reveals the wide-stretching landscape, but not if we close our eyes .... The whole universe is sacramental, but only if we are spiritually awake."[2] The Centurion, outsider that he was, had his eyes open. He was spiritually aware. Whereas the insiders, the religious types, were puffed up with intellectual pride, blinded with the cataracts of conceit.

Irony of ironies, surprise of surprises: the outsiders are in, the insiders are out; the wise are humbled, the humble are made wise; the powerful are made weak, the weak are made powerful; the righteous became sinners, the sinners became righteous; the first are last, and the last are first. Faith is found in unlikely people.

---

1. Bonhoeffer, Dietrich. "Good Death?" *Time,* March 10, 1975, Vol. 105, p. 84.

2. Major, Manson, and Wright. *The Mission And Message Of Jesus,* (New York: E. P. Dutton and Co., Inc., 1961), p. 692.

Ordinary Time 10
Luke 7:11-17

How To Rise Above Discouragement

It's a dramatic scene when you think about it — I mean — a funeral procession halted and the trip to the cemetery interrupted. Of course it was not anything like our scene — a black Cadillac hearse, followed by one or more black Cadillac limousines, followed perhaps by several cars, lights on, concerned not to lose their place in the line in the traffic.

No, this scene was at once more primitive and personal. No city traffic to contend with in this procession. No indifferent motorists disturbed that they were delayed a few minutes for the funeral. No, this is a village scene, people on foot, following the widowed mother who is following the professional mourners with their cymbals, flutes and high-pitched shrieking and wailing.

It is a Palestinian village scene in Nain, just a short distance from Nazareth (Jesus' hometown), and a day's walk from Capernaum (Jesus' new, adopted town). The pallbearers are carrying the body of a young man in a long wicker basket covered by a shroud for burial outside the city. Except for very important people, ancient Jews buried their dead outside the city, usually on the day of death or the next day. Embalming was not practiced.

For modern, indifferent eyes and blasé people, the scene was dramatic enough by itself. Think of it: the dead man was the only son of his mother, and she was a widow. The pathos and sorrow of the ages is contained in that statement, for in a patriarchal society orphans, of which he was one, and widows, which she was, were regarded as vulnerable, weak and without much opportunity for economic support. Nonetheless, a great crowd followed the procession, indicating sympathy and support at least for the time being.

That's drama enough — a large crowd of caring people — but now there is more. Jesus approaches, apparently coming from Capernaum where he just healed the Roman Centurion's slave. He saw the widowed, desolate mother, had compassion for her, thinking perhaps of his own mother reputedly widowed at an early age.

"Do not weep," he told her. Her tears for her son no doubt now intermingling with the endless salty tears shed for her husband. And in the continuing drama risking ceremonial impurity, he reached out, touched the bier and possibly the body, and the procession halted.

Can you see the modern setting — someone halting the hearse, opening the door of the limousine, telling the widowed mother in mourning black not to weep, and then saying beside the coffin, "Young man, I say to you, arise." Startling indeed, and startling enough in first century Palestine which had a tradition of miracle stories of great prophets like Elijah and Elisha raising widows' sons from the dead. And the young man sat up and began to speak, and like Elijah and Elisha before Jesus, the new great prophet gave the son back to his mother.

Talk about rising above discouragement! Talk about overcoming the greatest obstacle to human fulfillment. Talk about overcoming life's defeats: this was it — Jesus raising this young man from the dead as he had Jairus' daughter and Lazarus, brother of Mary and Martha.

He didn't raise everybody physically from the dead of course, just as he didn't heal everybody. But what he did do then and still does today, is to help everyone rise above discouragement. And that's where we focus today — rising above discouragement.

How do we rise above discouragement? For one thing we *do not deny the reality of our trouble.*

Biblical scholar William Barclay says, "We live in a world of broken hearts." Indeed we do. Any daily newspaper recounts tragic story after story of premature deaths, fractured relationships, and broken dreams. Indeed, we need not turn to any newspaper for an accounting of the world's troubles and sorrows. We have only to look at our own friends and neighbors and families. We have only to look into our own lives and hearts.

Jesus, the healer and power-giver, never insulted people by telling them their problems weren't real. He never told the sick they were never really sick or that their illness had no pain or reality. He never told people that death wasn't real, nor did he offer this widowed mother pollyanish pabulum to soothe her grieving heart.

I am reminded of a friend of mine living in Indiana where tornadoes are frequent. His young son had a special fear of storms. One day, when a storm threatened, the father took his son to the front of their lovely, substantial home, pointed out across the neighborhood, and said to the boy, "There, you see everything is okay. These are solid homes and we are safe and dry in them."

About that time a tornado touched down a block away and utterly destroyed several of these "substantial" homes. The storms of the natural world are real just as are the storms of the spiritual, psychological world. Trouble and tragedy are real. Evil and death are real. Jesus never said to his disciples on the stormy Sea of Galilee, "This is no storm. The storm is in your mind." He never said that. Instead he said to the storm, "Peace, be still." And it was.

Are you out of a job? Did your home decline in value? Are your financial resources dwindling? Do you have a serious illness? Is your marriage not right? Is there a real problem with the children? Are you enslaved in a debilitating habit? Then don't deny it, says Jesus. The widow never said her son wasn't dead. Admit the problems. Don't deny them. That's the first step in overcoming discouragement.

How are we to rise above discouragement? *We need to have the courage to consider alternatives.*

A few years ago in another city I was counselling a woman in a very troubled marriage. Over the course of several counselling sessions she recited in great detail the woes of her marriage and the faults and foibles of her spouse. The problems were real and she was indeed a very unhappy woman.

But when it came to considering alternatives, she was close-minded. Her husband was abusive and would not, under any circumstances, consider counselling. "Why not get a separation or divorce?" I asked. She couldn't for the sake of their child. "But the child is almost grown and gone, and besides he thinks you should get out of the relationship," I said.

She then stated she could not afford to move out. "But," I said, "you already are gainfully employed, and from what you have told me, earn quite a good income." "But," she replied, "without his income, I would have to live at a lower level than that to which I have become accustomed."

And so it went. She was indeed very unhappy in the marriage and had been for a long time. She was very discouraged, even to the point of despair, and perhaps even flirted once in a while with the thought of suicide. And yet she refused seriously to consider any alternative to her current situation.

Or here is a man about to lose his job due to large lay-offs in his company. He has two cars, a large mortgage, kids in school and one in college. The job market is tough, but his company does help him in outplacement, but in an area of the country which is not as appealing and which is some distance from his mother and father on whom he is quite dependent. So he turns down the outplacement and is faced with probable personal bankruptcy. He's greatly discouraged, but is so in large measure because he refused seriously to consider real alternatives.

I see this over and over again. People come to a dead end in marriage or job or self-understanding and then refuse to consider alternatives. They often refuse to consider alternatives because they want the future to be just like the past. They are afraid of adjustment or change. They have forgotten the words to James Russell Lowell's famous hymn:

New occasions teach new duties,
  Time makes ancient good uncouth.
He must always up and onward,
  Who would keep abreast of truth.

But long before Lowell it was Jesus who told the sick, "Have faith, stand up and walk." It was Jesus who said to the blind man, "Do you want to see?" and he did. It was Jesus who said, "Take up your cross and follow me." It was Jesus who said, "If you have faith you can move mountains."

It was Jesus himself who refused to be defeated by circumstances. Instead, he considered alternative ways of thinking and acting. That's what made him such a revolutionary person.

Want to rise above discouragement? Then let go of the past, the dead-ends, the cul-de-sacs, and the corners you've painted yourself into, and consider the alternatives Christ is ready to show you.

How do we rise above discouragement? *We must allow ourselves to be touched by Christ, by the transcendent, by the Divine Reality which is greater than ourselves.*

One of the surest ways to discouragement and death is to assume that all reality begins and ends with you. A lady of my acquaintance believes if she hasn't thought of it, it isn't true; or if she hasn't experienced it, it hasn't happened. The whole of reality is therefore defined by her narrow perceptions.

The late Jacob Bronowski, outstanding scientist with the Salk Institute, illustrated that truth in the world of science. He did a popular television series which he later put into a book titled, *The Ascent of Man* — a book which chronicled the development of scientific knowledge and understanding.

In the chapter having to do with knowledge and certainty, Bronowski confesses and laments how arrogant science had at one time become. He said he remembered when scientists thought they were on the verge of discovering the key to all reality, when suddenly a new discovery would open up a whole new world, and reality would lurch away from them into infinity. He then added we should avoid all arrogant, dogmatic stances with respect to knowledge, and say in the words of Oliver Cromwell, "By the mercies of Christ think it possible ye might be mistaken."

Invariably, when people become discouraged, they have allowed their own world and self-understanding to collapse in around them. Many discouraged and despairing people are suffocating in their own conceit. They get caught in the grip of doubt and refuse to doubt their own doubts; they refuse to question their own stale definitions of self and reality.

In contrast to this, Jesus calls us to open up to the Divine in prayer and humility. Or in the words of yesteryear's skeptic, Thomas Huxley, we need to say with him, "The longer I live, the more obvious it is to me that the most sacred act of a man's life is to say and to feel, 'I believe.' " That's what Harry Emerson Fosdick, the famous preacher of Riverside Church, New York City, had to do. Called to pastor and build that big church backed by the Rockefeller family and fortune, Fosdick eventually had a nervous breakdown.

"It was," said Fosdick, "the most terrifying wilderness I ever traveled through. I dreadfully wanted to commit suicide but instead made some of the most vital discoveries of my life. My little book, *The Meaning of Prayer*, would never have been written without that breakdown. I found God in a desert." Like Huxley, Fosdick could feel and say, "I believe."

We are forever learning that God is *for* us, not against us. It is we who are against ourselves in our myopia, our rigidity, our fear, our arrogance and stubbornness. Many of us are slow learners. We refuse to allow God to touch us with the new idea, the new self-understanding, the new job, the new opportunity, the new vital power he has to give.

It was Isaiah the prophet who put it so well for the Lord:

> *Seek the Lord while he may be found*
> *Call upon him while he is near ...*
> *For my thoughts are not your thoughts,*
> *neither are your ways my ways,*
> *says the Lord.*
> *For as the heavens are higher*
> *than the earth,*
> *so are my ways higher*
> *than your ways*
> *and my thoughts than your thoughts.*
> *(Isaiah 55:6, 8-9)*

It was the Divine Power which spoke to the dead young man that day long ago in the village of Nain. It was a dramatic sight, a rarity with Elijah, Elisha, Jesus and perhaps a few other great prophets. We shall have to wait until the end of time to see the grand resurrection of the dead.

But in our time and in all time, the power of the living Christ raises people up from discouragement, despondency, despair and from death itself. The Bible and books of the world and the churches are full of stories of how God helped and helps people rise above discouragement. And as Jesus said to that young man in Nain long ago, so would he say to each of us today, "Young man or old, young woman or old, I say to you, arise."

And you will.

Ordinary Time 11
Luke 7:36-50

Dinner Parties With A Difference

Religious leaders have had varying attitudes regarding dinner parties. Take John the Baptist, for instance. It is unlikely you would ever have gotten him inside a fine house around a beautiful table of exquisite crystal and china and gourmet food. That rustic, ascetic outdoorsman probably would have thought it a waste of time and money, an unnecessary frill to the essentials of life.

Many men today call themselves "meat and potatoes" men. No fancy foods for them. Just the basics. Forget all the fuss and bother. They just like a good steak, salad and potato. Let's sit down and eat and get it over with. But John the Baptist was even more rigid than that. Locusts and wild honey were his daily fare. No fine cuts of meat. No good dairy products. No wine touched his lips. Fasting and prayer and preaching were his daily regimen. He couldn't waste time with the frills and pleasures of a dinner party.

Jesus was different; so different in fact, he had the religious people of his day chattering about his behavior. Aside from the time of his wilderness temptation experiences, Jesus apparently avoided the ascetic way of life. Unlike John who scorned polite society, Jesus seemed to enjoy being with people on a wide variety of social occasions. He turned the water into wine at the wedding feast in Cana. He dined often with friends like Mary, Martha and Lazarus. Matthew and Zacchaeus each had a large feast with Jesus as an honored guest. Today's scripture describes him at yet another dinner party.

Consequently, rumors began to fly. People were wondering just how religious Jesus was. The followers of John the Baptist were inquiring about Jesus' behavior, wondering why he didn't fast more frequently. It looked to them as though he were enjoying life far too much. Jesus attended dinner parties so often, his enemies even accused him of being a glutton and drunkard.

I must confess I much prefer Jesus' behavior to John's, although I believe occasional fasting and much prayer to be good for the soul. I must also confess that many church people prefer their minister to behave more like John than Jesus. It is true, of course, that I probably could make people feel much more guilty if I were thinner, my face more austere and my eyes squintier. Any minister who looks as though he enjoys *this* life a lot has a hard time convincing his flock to prepare for the *next* life.

More than once I have been enjoying myself at dinner parties only to have people look at me quizzically as if to say, "You're a minister. Don't you know any better? You're not supposed to be having such a good time." On other occasions I have been seated at a feast with people of perhaps questionable reputation, only to have others wonder why I would be associating with that crowd. I myself sometimes have wondered that. Nevertheless, I'm usually willing to go about anywhere to grab someone for the kingdom of God, hoping in the meantime they don't grab me.

Jesus loved dinner parties. In fact, the early Christians had lots of them after Jesus' ascension. As they met together in the evening for their love feasts, their fellowship suppers, they broke their bread together in thanksgiving and memory of Jesus. And as they lifted the cup of wine, they thanked God for Jesus' life-blood, and remembered how his life literally had been poured out for them.

These early Christians were not being irreverent. Rather they were fulfilling Jesus' request that they remember him at their dinner parties. Communion is a remnant of those early feasts. We have only token amounts of bread and wine. But it's Jesus' dinner party nevertheless, and his table. He is the host; we are the guests. However, unlike the feast at Simon's house, Jesus' feast is a dinner party with a difference.

Jesus' dinner party is different because he includes people who do not seem to be his own kind.

The Pharisee had invited Jesus on the belief that he was a prophet, but that idea was dispelled when Jesus failed to discern that the woman touching him was a prostitute. The customary understanding of a prophet was tinged with the Pharisee's idea of separatism, of holiness touching no unclean thing. Thus, if Jesus were a holy prophet, he surely would not have let this intimate touching proceed.

When we gather around Jesus' table, his supper, his spiritual feast, it is surprising how many people gather at his table with an attitude more like that of Simon the Pharisee, than that of Jesus. Simon wanted at his table only those who were as pure and as good as he conceived himself to be. He was insulted Jesus would besmirch his high quality feast with apparent acceptance and recognition of such a low quality woman.

Today, many followers of Jesus regrettably have switched to the mentality of Simon. They believe only persons of the highest quality and most sanctified holiness are welcome at the table. Simon and his friends believed they had earned the right to associate together to celebrate their status and goodness. And indeed they had. They were good people. They gave alms, prayed every day, fasted twice a week, and supported temple and synagogue with the tithe, which meant ten percent before taxes. Furthermore, they kept up to date on their religious teachings, even to the minutest detail of their religious law. If anyone had earned the right to belong to an exclusive dinner party, they had. Without dispute, they were good men.

The prostitute had led quite a different life. Somewhere in her past, she may have been sexually abused, or she may have lacked love, or may have fallen into self-loathing, and then desperately sought some kind of warmth or affection. Or it might be she was trying, in her own way, to conquer a male-chauvinist, double-standard society. If she had been widowed or divorced, she might have turned to the only means of livelihood open to her in those days.

We can assume she gave few alms. Fasting would not be good for her profession. Attendance at religious services was rare. She might have sent a holiday gift to the temple or synagogue as a kind of guilt offering. But she was not the kind of person priests and rabbis could count on for solid support of their religious institutions. Mothers attempted to shield their daughters from this woman's influence. Wives hoped their husbands never would fall into her seductive traps. But even the priests and rabbis had to acknowledge that somewhere out there, men were giving her business, perhaps even good men.

Are there any good men here today? Are there any bad women here today? Who then is welcome at Jesus' table?

Christians with Pharisaic attitudes like those of Simon believe only the good people should gather at the table, that only the worthy should come to Christ's dinner party. His feast, they claim, is only for those who have "arrived" religiously. Those of lesser religious and moral status politely should excuse themselves.

Not so, says Jesus. Untrue. Unlike dinner parties which are called to enhance our mutual admiration society, my dinner party is different, says Jesus. So long as you come openly with faith and repentance as did this woman, you are welcome. I accept you. I want to include you among my friends. I will forgive you if you are willing to give up your phoniness, to lay it straight, to come clean, admitting your wrongs.

I realize, says Jesus, that you may feel as though you are not up to my standards, that you feel you may not know how to behave in my circle of friends. But that really doesn't matter. In fact, it's that kind of feeling that qualifies you more than anything else. The truth is, my people are not really all that good. They're sinners just like you, and they know it and confess it. They came to my feast to receive my acceptance and the encouragement of my other followers. Surprisingly, the way to be admitted is to admit you are not worthy. True humility gets you everywhere.

There is another difference in the dinner party of Jesus. *It encourages genuine interest in the other person.*

I read once of a super salesman going to lunch at the fashionable Delmonico's in New York's Wall Street district. As he entered the busy restaurant and walked across the crowded dining room behind the maitre'd, he purposely knocked a glass-laden tray out of a waiter's hand. Within a split second every executive eye in the place was on the super salesman who drank in the attention, hoping he would never be forgotten. Other salesmen by the hundreds came and went to Delmonico's unnoticed, but not this man. He wanted to call attention to himself, to gain recognition and thus potential customers.

Most of us enter fashionable restaurants more modestly, if not more timidly, than that salesman. Nevertheless, as we gather with friends and acquaintances, our egos may be just as large and starved as his. Some people go to dinner parties to impress rather than be impressed, to talk rather than to listen, to be confirmed in their prejudices rather than to be changed.

Notice the difference between Simon and the prostitute. Simon was cold and calculating, the prostitute warm and receptive. Simon, in his self-centeredness, unforgivably had forgotten the common courtesies of mid-eastern hospitality of washing guests' feet and greeting them with an embrace and kiss. The prostitute washed Jesus' feet with her tears, dried them with her hair, and rubbed costly ointment on them. Simon, in a position to be generous, was selfish and censorious. The poor woman, in a position to be selfish, was generous and loving. Simon was thinking of himself. The woman was thinking of Jesus.

The most exciting dinner parties I have attended are those where people genuinely are interested in one another. The most disappointing are those where everyone is playing one-upmanship, or where people are blasé and really not open to one another.

Writing in *Harper's* magazine, Peter Marin once suggested our country is characterized by the latter mentality more than the former. There is a new narcissism in the land, says Marin. Self-love has been elevated to the ultimate. Genuine human community and reciprocity are lacking. It is so easy for the self to replace a sense of community or genuine relationship with others or with God. Thus we lose any sense of the real presence of another self, and with it, our sense of identity and reciprocal relationship. There is no give and take, only take.

Do you see what was happening with the prostitute? For the first time in her life she truly was loving somebody. Until recently she had been exploiting men in the name of love. In reality it was a vicious circle of exploitation and hate, each person using the other for his or her selfish gratification. The startling thing about Jesus was that he looked at her in a way no other man looked. He looked beyond her body to her soul, beyond her external glamour to her interior heart. He was not looking for bargain basement love. Rather he was looking at a self in need of genuine human feeling and acceptance and forgiveness.

Simon, on the other hand, was really in the exploitative frame of mind. He had Jesus over to dinner more or less to test his credentials to see if he might "fit in" or if he might possibly be used for the Pharisees' cause. He cared little for Jesus as a person, except as he might enhance or threaten the Pharisees' position. No real community took place between Jesus and Simon. Simon wasn't open. His was the old narcissism, forever becoming new.

The joy of true community took place between Jesus and the woman because they were thinking of each other. They focused on each other's needs and thus genuinely were fulfilled. Look at that picture again. Can you imagine yourself washing Jesus' feet and kissing them? Or drying them with your hair? Who of us would humble ourselves to do that for anybody?

So often we come to take from Jesus, not to give. We want peace of mind, strength for living, success in business, support for our latest cause. But first we must come to give — to give him our love, our honor, our allegiance, our need for forgiveness. Then when we know that we have been forgiven much, perhaps we can love much, and his dinner party will indeed be different from any we have experienced.

Ordinary Time 12
Luke 8:26-39

Demons, Pigs
And The Economy

In polite society we have not wanted to talk much of demons and the demonic. In our liberal, educated culture, we have believed that sin was due mostly to ignorance and that evil could be eradicated by education. In our psychologically enlightened times we have avoided the more ancient religious and mythological language of devils and evil. We have instead preferred words like repression, impulses, sublimation, drives, complexes, phobias, regression, neuroses, psychoses, manic-depressive, schizophrenic and schizoid — to name a few.

If we have been suspicious of religious healers and exorcists and spiritual counselors, we have been implicitly trustful of psychiatrists, psychologists, psychoanalysts, counselors and therapy groups. If we have been doubtful of prayer, meditation and conversion, we have been trustful of amphetamines, barbiturates and tranquilizers, not to mention alcohol, cocaine, and marijuana. If in our time witch doctors have disappeared, strangely enough witches have reappeared by the thousands. Even exorcists are making a small comeback after considerable media exposure and hype.

Whether demons and the demonic are widely acknowledged in our time may be debated, but that they were common in Jesus' time we can have no doubt. In his time, when most illness was attributable to sin, it was but a short step to attribute all mental illness or epilepsy to demonic powers actually residing in the person and controlling him or her. Thus to cure a person of seizures or dementia or schizophrenia or melancholia, the healer had to have power not only to name the demon, but power to cast him out, to throw him out of the center of the person's self.

In the ancient world, demons were almost beyond number. They could inhabit almost any living thing and take control. More than that, the demons, and especially the prince of the demons, the devil, were thought actually to have the world under their control.

Thus, not only could physical and mental illness be attributed to them; catastrophes and disasters and evil events of all sorts should be attributed to their power. Therefore, if one was to gain control of human life and history, one had to contend with demons and devils, to wrestle with "the powers of darkness of this present world" as Paul put it.

It is no wonder then that the early church was fascinated with this intriguing story of Jesus and the Gerasene demoniac. Mark's version of the story is probably the original. Matthew names two demoniacs in place of one. And Luke, the beloved physician, emphasizes the state of mind before and after the healing or exorcism. More than that, as the only non-Jewish writer of the New Testament, Luke likes to emphasize Jesus' interest in all people, including Gentiles. (For this exorcism takes place in Gentile territory and the cured man is asked to bear witness to his healing among the Gentiles.)

The early church was fascinated with this powerful story, and so are we. For if we are to have healthy lives and a healthy economy, we shall have to deal with our demons.

Let us consider the demoniac. We may understand him more than we realize.

The gospels tell us he lived in the carved-out caves or tombs near the Sea of Galilee. Ostracized from society because of his initial mental illness, the demoniac's condition is exacerbated by society's total rejection. Wild in his efforts to resist rejection and exclusion, the authorities chain him down at both hands and feet.

But in a surge of frightened, defiant, maniacal strength, he refuses to be entrapped in the ancient equivalent of a straitjacket. He bursts the bonds, ripping off his clothes as a rejection of all constriction and runs wildly among the rocks, shrieking and screaming obscenities at the unjust, uncaring, hypocritical world, bruising and cutting himself in the process.

Thus it is with considerable courage that Jesus comes into the presence of this terrifying creature. If the ancient equivalent of a tourist bus might have come within viewing distance of this "local attraction," none, out of fear for their lives, dared confront this maniac.

No one except Jesus. Jesus, the integrated man; Jesus, the man in whom the centering-in powers of the universe found a home; Jesus, in whom the healing powers of God were focused; Jesus, the prayerful man at peace with God and with himself; this Jesus, calm, strong and fearless, approached the frantic, frenetic, disintegrated man with faith and assurance.

Rather than pouncing on Jesus and tearing him to shreds, the deranged demoniac, with the highly charged, sensitized, inward vision of the psychotic — this frenzied, distorted intelligence — falls down before Jesus, and cries out, "What have you to do with me, Jesus, son of the Most High God? I beseech you, do not torment me."

The flailing, frantic, disintegrated man sensed he was in the presence and power of someone whole and integrated; someone controlled more by faith than fear; someone more loving than defensive; someone more accepting than judgmental; yet someone who would not patronize him or trivialize his illness or belittle his lack of strength to cope with the powers that had gained control of his very being. "Jesus, Son of God Most High, what do you have to do with me?" And the answer was, and is, everything.

He has everything to do with societies torn apart by the demonic.

No doubt most of us would resist being called demoniacs, and many of us would hesitate to allow that our society might be demonic. Nonetheless, the more sensitive and perceptive among us see swirling powers and forces in our midst that threaten to take control of us and destroy us. The forces of disintegration and fragmentation make it more and more difficult to hold ourselves together. Are there not times, as one person told me, when we are ready to strip off our civilized clothes and run into the wilderness shrieking primal screams of utter despair.

If the demoniac was a schizophrenic, ours is often a schizoid, divided life, says popular psychoanalyst and author, Rollo May. Like the demoniac, we feel more and more alone, more and more empty, more and more rejected, more and more forgotten, passed by and neglected. More than that, our inward self seems diminished.

Consequently, as Dr. May observed, "When the inward life dries up, when feeling decreases and apathy increases, when one cannot affect or even genuinely *touch* another person, violence flares up as a demoniac necessity for contact, a mad drive forcing touch in the most direct way possible."[1]

Like the demoniac thrust out of society into the caves and rocks, we seem thrust out of selfhood in an impersonal, institutionalized, systematized, bureaucratic society. How many of us have had to rage at another company's computer only to install one in our own company against which our customers rage? And if we think talking with a business or company is bad, try talking with the government or the Internal Revenue Service where you are assumed guilty until proven innocent.

In a society where we feel oppressed or powerless, in a system where we feel inconsequential and exploited, in a culture which seems controlled by alien forces, we react like the demoniac in violence or distorted sexuality. In an effort to touch someone, in a craving to know and to be known, in an effort to be something more than a social security number on an IRS form, in our struggle to be more than upper middle class serfs to a government despicably wasteful — in such an effort, is it any wonder we react in violence and distorted sexuality in a desperate effort to feel, to be connected, to count somehow and to make a difference?

Our schizoid world may not be far from that of the demoniac's. If artists and neurotics are predictive and prophetic as Dr. May suggests, Picasso's painting, *Guernica,* with its fragmented bulls and torn villages of modern war, is predictive. The atrocities of the Viet Nam War, the wasted lives, the utter, barbaric brutality, the waste, the disorder, the lack of discipline, the drug addiction and mental derangement — the smoke and blood of real battle on our televisions during our cocktail hour — all this was a symbol of the disjointedness and disintegration of our own society, a society not unlike that of the demoniac.

So in the ancient despair we shriek, "Jesus, Son of the Most High God, what do you have to do with us?" And he answers firmly and quietly, "What is your name?" We reply, "Legion," for like the ancient demoniac who may have gone berserk after witnessing the horrible atrocities of war, we too experience 6,000 demons like a legion of Roman soldiers exerting terrible power and influence over us and our society.

But then Jesus says, "Come out of him, come out of them." In the context of the church, in the surroundings of the worshipping community, amid a people committed to wholeness and balance, to saneness and integration, amidst a people singing and praying and centering on God in faith, hope and love — in such a context, the powerful, peaceable voice of Jesus is heard, saying, "Come out of them, you negative, destructive demonic power. Come out of them you oppressive ideas, you controlling compulsions and obsessions. Come out of them you powers of guilt and regret and revenge. Come out of them you faulty self-images and harmful habits. Release them. Let them go. Be healed. Peace be with you."

And Jesus comes again and again, making his assault on demoniacs and demonic societies, making them whole and

and peaceful and integrated. Christ's gospel, says historian T. R. Glover, "took terror out of men's souls ... and greatly purified and sweetened life."[2] Whenever the church returns to him there is a resurrection, says Dr. Glover, an evidence of new life. As the demoniac was made whole, so might we be.[3]

But if Jesus has power to heal demonic societies, *he also has power to change economies.*

When you think of it, there may have been some humor in this story. Consider this: Jesus, a practicing Jew, consorting among Gentiles who, of all things, were raising forbidden pigs for non-kosher pork. Even more ironic, it may have been some back-sliding Jews who were raising the forbidden pigs to sell at good profit to the neighboring Gentiles.

So, when looking for a place to put the 6,000 demons, Jesus honored the demons' request to go into 2,000 pigs (that's three demons per pig). Now demon-possessed, the pigs, in a demonic frenzy, run off the cliff into the lake and drown. So much for the forbidden pigs and non-kosher pork. At least, thought the more faithful and orthodox Jews, the pigs were put to good use!

The economic question here is, is a man worth 2,000 pigs? The former demoniac is now sitting calmly at Jesus' feet, clothed, sane, whole, peaceful, ready to lead a productive life as Jesus' disciple to the Gentiles. Think of it — from demoniac to disciple. But the herdsmen, thinking of the lost pigs, ran into the city to tell the owners. They in turn came rushing out to the scene. In disbelief they saw the wild demoniac they had rejected and chained, now sitting peaceably and calmly in his right mind. They were amazed.

But then another reality took hold of them — the reality of lost ham, bacon and pork chops! I don't know how many of you trade in hogs and pork bellies, but I recently noticed hog futures were about 48 cents per pound. So for a herd of hogs at an average of 150 pounds per hog, those 2,000 pigs were worth about $144,000 by today's prices! Is it worth

2,000 pigs or $144,000 to cure one demoniac? What if the pigs belonged to you or me?

But what if the demoniac was your son, the Viet Nam veteran, or your father, or your deranged husband, or your disturbed brother or mine? Is it worth $144,000 to make a man well? What price shall we put on a man? Shall economic factors be the sole values by which we adjudge life or death?

Should we care more for dollars or for people? If *our* pigs had been lost, would we have focused more on them than on the man made whole? And would we, like the Gerasenes, ask Jesus to leave our city, our country, our economy? Have we? One scholar quips sadly, "All down the ages the world has been refusing Jesus because it prefers pigs."[4]

In a recent lecture the popular author, Christopher Lasch, wonders about the lack of morality and human values in our society. Many liberals today, says Lasch, see public life as an amoral struggle for profit and power and relegate morality to the shadowy realm of private choice and "lifestyles." What we need, says Lasch, is a new sense of fraternalism, a new sense of brotherhood that is neither self-righteous nor exploitative. To bring more peace and wholeness we need to cast out the demons of greed and exploitation and indifference.

When Jesus comes into an area, he not only casts out demons, he changes the economy because he changes people, their goals and values. When Paul preached Christ's gospel in ancient Ephesus, the silversmiths and others, who made religious souvenirs and idols of the goddess, Diana, knew their economy was in trouble if Jesus' religion flourished.

John Newton, author of "Amazing Grace," finally stopped his slave trading when Jesus really got hold of his life. Charles Colson, Richard Nixon's hatchet man, was converted and now devotes his life to prison reform. What would happen to our frenetic age of greed if Jesus really got hold of the bankers and financiers and politicians who have broken so many laws, lost so much money, and burdened the average American taxpayer with several thousands of dollars of debt?

Make no mistake about it: in the name of God, Jesus is interested in fraternalism, in brotherhood, and in an economy that serves people and that enables as many people as possible to share in the world's fabulous wealth. Jesus' intent is not to bring us all to poverty but to bring us all the abundant life. And in economies which break the back of the poor to fill the stock portfolios of the rich, would not Jesus call for reform? In economies where a very small percentage of people own the greatest share of property, would he not call for reform?

In military dictatorships where the individual is little more than "cannon fodder" for the megalomania of the ruler, would he not call for reform? In a society like ours where the government no longer exists to serve the citizens, but the citizens exist to serve the government, would not Jesus call for reform? And in societies where the rich get richer, the poor get poorer, and the middle class gets increasingly squeezed out, would not Jesus call for reform?

In all economies, rich or poor, would not Jesus call for brotherly, humane, creative ways to care for the mentally ill, the developmentally disabled, the homeless and helpless and emotionally distressed? And in a society too quickly and easily given over to the dollar sign, would not Jesus call us again to the worship of the Most High God who has power to cast out all demons and to make us whole?

May Jesus ever prevail over demons, pigs and the economy — and us.

---

1. May, Rollo. *Love And Will,* (New York: W. W. Norton and Co., 1969), p. 30-31.

2. Glover, T.R. *Jesus In The Experience Of Men,* (London: Student Christian Movement, 1921), p. 7.

3. *Ibid.,* p. 13.

4. Levertoff as quoted by R.V.G. Tasher. *Matthew: Tyndale New Testament Commentaries,* (Grand Rapids, Michigan: William B. Eerdman's Publishing Co), p. 94.

Ordinary Time 13
Luke 9:51-62

A New Kingdom Coming

A lot of people don't believe it — but there's a new kingdom coming. Nevertheless, there is a new kingdom coming. Often, like a phoenix bird, it arises out of the ashes of the old. As a young sapling is germinated by forest fire, so the new kingdom is sprouted in the desolation of despair. Like tundra flowers and crab grass the new kingdom has irresistible life impulses and grows anywhere. There is a new kingdom coming.

You may wonder where it is — this new kingdom. You may look for advance press releases, television bulletins, screaming headlines. Or you may listen for the voice of battle, the clamor of war, the sound of trumpets. And you will look and listen in vain, for this kingdom comes as leaven in loaves overflowing bread pans, as new wine fermentation bursting old wineskins, as tiny mustard seeds gently growing to giant stalks. The kingdom has been coming, is here among us, and is coming still.

During World War II there arose an unexplainable shortage of chewing gum in the Pacific theater. The mystery soon was solved. American airplanes dropped billions of sticks of chewing gum over enemy-occupied Philippines. And on the inside of every gum wrapper these words were printed: "I shall return. MacArthur."

Although there is a shortage of natural chicle for chewing gum (they're using a plastic substitute), there is no shortage of gum wrappers. We ought to acquire them and drop them all over our "enemy-occupied" world with these words on them: "I shall return. Jesus."

In the midst of our current pessimism and enslaving despair, we are here to announce a new kingdom coming. We have a liberator, a King whose kingdom is coming, the hope for which lifts us above the delusions of fading temporal power.

Note first of all, *the new kingdom coming is out of the future, not the past.*

Many Americans are amused at the quaintness of the Amish people. These descendants of Germanic pietism attempt to stop the clock, to idealize a segment of time as the kingdom of God. Almost wholly agricultural, they ride about their farms and towns in horse-drawn vehicles, avoid the modern conveniences of electricity, and disdain any instruction other than that of their own schools. For them, the ideal of the kingdom of God seems to be fixed somewhere around mid-19th century.

Riding about in modern automobiles with modern dress, many of us are more similar to the Amish than we like to believe. The ideal life, the ideal church, the ideal family was somewhere in the past for some of us. Consequently we keep looking over our shoulders at some period of the past like Adam and Eve looking over their shoulders at the Garden of Eden on their way out. If only we could return to the good old days!

Indeed, there may have been better days in the past. And we may be greatly distressed with the present. But the kingdom of God is coming out of the future. And if we insist on horse and buggy faith we may miss the rocket realities of the new age. Throughout Biblical history God has been leading people out of past bondage and bondage to the past. He led Abraham out of Ur, Israel out of Egypt, Judah out of Babylonia, mankind out of hades and death. The past belongs to fewer and fewer people. The future belongs to everybody.

Ed Coale, Chief Executive Officer of General Motors, retired a few years ago after 44 years with one of the world's leading corporations. Perched at the pinnacle of American career success with a large compensation in salary and bonuses, Coale said the happiest day of his life was when he left G.M. When asked if he would do it again, he answered no.

Why this bitterness from one who had reached the rarefied atmosphere of the pyramid-top Camelot? "It's no fun anymore," said Coale. "Governmental regulations are immense and burdensome. There's an awful lot of enterprise in America," said Coale. "But because of governmental intervention, very little of it is free enterprise."

If Coale was displeased with the burdensome future created by Washington legislators and bureaucrats, others are dismayed at the future created by technocrats such as Coale in the automotive industry. Even now, the new anti-pollutant catalytic converter will itself pollute our air with dangerous quantities of sulfuric acid.

Future Shock author, Alvin Toffler, is correct when he says: "Technocrats suffer from myopia. Their instinct is to think about immediate returns, immediate consequences. They are premature members of the now generation."[1]

Further, says Toffler, "To plan for a more distant future does not mean to tie oneself to dogmatic programs .... It means an infusion of the entire society, from top to bottom, with a new socially aware future-consciousness."[2]

Christians have had, for centuries, a future consciousness, when they have talked of Christ's kingdom coming, a kingdom never yet fully realized or actualized, but always in the process of becoming in each successive stage of history. It is when Christians walk backward into history with eyes fixed on the dogmatisms of the past, that the kingdom's forward march is frustrated. Some Christians have to be dragged, kicking and screaming, into the future. This is not to say the past is unimportant. It is only to say it is less important, because it belongs to fewer and fewer people. The future belongs to everybody.

Alvin Toffler maintains we need more than ever a creative group to imagine a whole array of possible and preferable futures. Rather than ridiculing new ideas we must remember, "the essence of creativity is a willingness to play the fool, to toy with the absurd, only later submitting the stream of ideas to harsh critical judgment .... We need," Toffler continues, "sanctuaries for social imagination."[3]

And I ask, what better sanctuary than this and tens of thousands like it around the earth where we can dream dreams and see visions for the better future into which God would lead us? After all, for centuries Christianity has not only stimulated the imagination — it has followed its vision to the pain of death.

John Wycliffe had a vision of a Bible in the common English tongue. But dogmatists anchored to the past killed him for it. John Huss dreamed a dream of a responsible Christian life guided by the scriptures. Traditionalists burned him at the stake. Martin Luther was awakened to a new reality of God's grace — an awakening not shared by contemporaries profiting from the status quo. Consequently, he was hunted for years for revealing an exciting and preferable future. A kingdom was coming and the powers of evil could not prevail against it.

Hundreds of thousands more could be named — dreamers and seers who envisioned a better future — God's future where justice is more just, a righteousness more right, love more sincere. And the question in any age is whether there is yet a people to dream God's dreams, a remnant to think his thoughts after him, seers to catch the vision. How many are there in this sanctuary of social imagination? How many in this place of God — this place of courage, erected in faith, sustained in prayer, enlivened by the Holy Spirit of God? How many? How many agents of the kingdom — a kingdom needing to come, wanting to come, waiting to come?

Note secondly, *the coming kingdom requires our mutual support — spiritual and physical.*

Very few people are expert in anything all by themselves. They need a supporting community. Do you know a good musician who was not trained, nurtured and sustained by the music community? Show me an athlete who achieves excellence all alone, apart from the athletic community. Very few wise men become so without the accumulated wisdom of the centuries as expressed in colleges and universities and libraries. Medical people are more like ensembles and symphonies than soloists. What business tycoon does it all on his own without dedicated experts in finance, engineering, personnel, and marketing? Excellence requires participation in, and support of, a community of like-minded people.

Likewise in the church — a forerunner of the new kingdom. Very few achieve Christian maturity all by themselves. Seldom is the Bible studied diligently without the aid of scholars and teachers. Rarely are people led to generosity by their own impulses. More often, the Spirit of Christ, pulsating in the church, opens up the doors of the selfish, stingy heart to take in the brother. After all, Silas Marner and Scrooge were lonely, hermit types. Generous saints are social saints.

One time a little Sunday school saint was greatly chagrined when her brother and sister received church letters inviting them to choir and Sunday school, and she didn't. At mail time next day, when her letters arrived, her face brightened and she exclaimed happily, "I guess they really want me over there." The church really does!

The new kingdom coming is at its heart spiritual, but it needs a lot of physical fuel. Flying airplanes is a great spiritual and psychological dream, but it quickly becomes a nightmare without gas. Education is a great adventure of the mind, but turn off the research money and teaching energy and cerebral arthritis will set in. The refined experiences of high culture rest heavily upon the sweat of custodians and craftsmen. Just as the soaring abstract realities of mind and thought depend upon the more apparent realities of blood, bones, and body, so too the high adventures of spirit depend upon the church as body, life-blood and skeletal bone.

The kingdom of God is materialistic. It's waiting for your material — your body, your brain, your energetic life-blood, your strong support. It has little to do with jelly-fish day dreams, idle thought or vain imagination. The kingdom coming has to do with reality — reality in all its dimensions, physical and spiritual.

One time a leading citizen of the community was selling season symphony tickets to his business friends, soliciting their support. One friend said, "Thanks a lot, John. I love music, and I think it's a grand idea for our community to have a fine orchestra. But no thanks on the tickets. However, we'll be with you in spirit." However, John was quick on the draw and replied, "Well, wonderful. And just how many tickets would your spirit like?"

Jesus said, "Why do you call me 'Lord, Lord,' and not do what I tell you?" (Luke 6:46). James says, "If a brother or sister is ill-clad and in lack of daily food, and one of you says to them, 'Go in peace, be warmed and filled,' without giving them the things needed for the body, what does it profit?" (James 2:15-16). Jesus says, "Not everyone who says to me, 'Lord, Lord' shall enter the kingdom of heaven, but he who does the will of my father who is in heaven" (Matthew 7:21).

How many tickets would you like for your spirit? The coming kingdom is waiting for you like the water reservoir is waiting for you to turn the faucet. Your closed faucet affects not the reservoir's reality, but yours. Like a mighty reservoir of justice and peace and love, God's kingdom is waiting for us to turn on the rusted faucet, waiting for us to cleanse the hardened arteries of constricted spirituality, to remove the plaque of selfishness, the corrosion of conceit. There's a new kingdom coming. It's waiting for you — for me.

Thirdly, this *new kingdom coming has a living, challenging King, not a dead one.*

Jesus said, "Follow me," not into the grave, but into life. But as German theologian/martyr Dietrich Bonhoeffer pointed out: "The object of Jesus' command is always the same — to evoke whole-hearted faith, to make us love God and our neighbor with all our heart and soul."[4]

When people begin to raise objections about the mission of the church, when they begin to balk at adequate financial sharing and contribution of time and talent, the problem nearly always is traceable to a lack of love. For as Paul says, "If you love someone you will always do the best for him." When we hesitate and balk at even the most basic of Christian responsibilities we should examine our hearts, for therein we shall find mixed affections and loyalties. When Christian tasks seem only irksome duty, we can be sure we have fixed our priorities on something else than the kingdom of God.

Like all great leaders and teachers, Jesus often has a problem with his followers. Karl Barth, the late well-known and influential theologian of Switzerland, once said, "I hope I shall never become a Barthian. May God spare me from Barthianism!" Barth didn't want to be hemmed in or trapped by the smallest of his own followers who wanted to package him, market him, and profit from him as a safe product. Unable to keep up with the living Barth, they preferred the static Barth of printed pages. That way they could possess Barth, hold him in their hands, control him, use him to buttress their own biases.

Many contemporary disciples use Jesus in a similar way. They like the Jesus of a book better than the living Jesus because they can control and manipulate a religious leader in print, use his words to buttress their biases. But let Jesus come alive, and you have unpredictable demands. He then is in control. He is the teacher and we are the students. He the master, we the servants.

But we don't like that. We want to be in charge. We like to be the chiefs, not the Indians, and call the shots. Jesus may cause us discomfort and inconvenience. He might pin us to the wall on our discomfort and inconvenience. He might pin us to the wall in our selfishness and hardness of heart. He might expose the silent glee we have when the church has problems raising a budget or launching a program. He may press the question, "If you're not on *my* side, just *whose* side *are* you on?" We may want to say, "Let me go tend my field, bury my father, seek my pleasure, pursue my happiness, build my nest egg," but he says, "Follow me."

In the medieval period parts of Europe often were characterized by feudal fiefdoms and provincial territories of crown princes. But to create a unified state, feudal lords and crown princes were persuaded or forced to swear allegiance to the king. The king knew once he had the loyalty and allegiance of individual lords, he would have their lands and powers, their energies and resources.

Likewise in the kingdom of God. We all build our provincial kingdoms of corporations, professions, families, houses and lands, over which we preside like feudal lords on manorial estates. But God's sovereignty is established only when, through his judgment and kindness, we surrender ourselves to his lordship. God knows when we put our own hearts and minds and spirits under his control, he then will have access to all we possess — our money, our abilities, our time. And Jesus is his vice-regent who bids us give the King our all for his great causes.

Nevertheless, afflicted with spiritual myopia, obsessed with the illusion of material things, shackled by a selfish heart, we resist the overtures of the Heavenly King and cling to our Dark Age feudal mentality. Unable to become immersed in the larger challenges and benefits of God, we become states' rights isolationists. Unaware of the immensely greater truths awaiting our discovery, blind to the larger vision of reality, insensitive to the suffering heart of the universe, we repulse the vice-regent and say, "I've got to tend my field," "I must wait until my father dies and then ...," "I really love these lands and my family too much to share them." And the King's vice-regent will say, "He who loves houses and lands and family more than me is not worthy of me." There's a new kingdom coming. Will you be a part of the union or remain a selfish, separatist state?

There's a new kingdom coming — coming out of the future — a kingdom needing to come, wanting to come, waiting to come. Waiting for you. For me. For this church, this nation, this world. "I will build my church," said Jesus, "and the gates of hell shall not prevail against it." Therefore, "thy kingdom come, thy will be done, on earth, as it is in heaven."

---

1. Toffler, Alvin. *Future Shock,* (New York: Random House, 1970), p. 406.

2. *Ibid.*

3. *Ibid.,* p. 411.

4. Bonhoeffer, Dietrich, *The Cost Of Discipleship,* (New York: Macmillan Co., 1966), p. 252.

Ordinary Time 14
Luke 10:1-12

How To Get
The Job Done

It's a startling fact but true — Jesus and politicians have a lot in common. This no doubt comes as a surprise to those who regard politics as a dirty business, or who think of politicians essentially as liars, and who believe steadfastly that politics and religion don't mix. Nonetheless, Jesus and the politicians have a lot in common.

When you think of it, politicians get elected by promising us something better. A few years ago President Reagan was elected and then re-elected by asking the public, "Are you better off now than four years ago?" The first time, the people answered, "no," and elected Reagan for the promise of something better. Four years later they responded "yes" to the question and elected Reagan for another term in hope for an even better four years.

Jesus and politicians do have a lot in common. Not always, however. A little girl asked her mother whether all fairy tales began with, "Once upon a time." "No," replied the mother. "Today most of them begin with 'If I'm elected.' " Jesus made promises, but not like that.

Was Jesus, 2,000 years ago, promising something better? Indeed he was. He said he had come to bring in the kingdom of God, the rules of God's righteousness in the world. For 900 years, Jews had been hoping for a restoration of the glorious kingdom of David and Solomon. For 500 years they had been longing for an end to foreign tyranny and a return to prosperity and freedom. And in Jesus' time the longings and expectations were at an all-time high.

For Jews of that time, the hopes of a better life were often focused on a Messiah, a new King David who would come and restore their good fortune. Others spoke of a messianic age about to arrive, the coming of the kingdom of God, a time when God would reign supreme over his people, and freedom and prosperity and the good life would be enjoyed. It would also be a time when righteousness and justice and peace would prevail.

Had there been people who claimed to be the promised Messiah? Indeed there had been, and the Romans, then occupying Judea and Palestine, promptly disposed of them. But now Jesus appears on the scene, announcing far and wide that the kingdom of God is at hand, and that he is God's agent to bring in his kingdom, the new and better life.

Not only is Jesus like politicians in promising a new and better way, he is like them in his struggle to get the word out to all the people, to announce the kingdom is coming, to raise expectations and to prepare them to receive Jesus' message. Without newspapers, radios and television, how do you get the job done? You do it in person and you delegate emissaries, advance men, to prepare the way and to excite anticipation for Jesus' arrival and for his message of hope.

Politicians could learn from Jesus, and so could businesses and churches. For would we not all agree, he got the job done! After all, one-fourth of today's world population, a billion plus people, claim to be Jesus' people. And that doesn't even count the millions who have preceded us in the previous 20 centuries.

How do we get the job done in our time? Our text gives us clues. Here they are.

The first thing we learn from Jesus is to *delegate*.

Delegation is more difficult than it sounds. Delegation is especially difficult for talented and extraordinary leaders, and even more difficult for leaders who seem to have a special calling from God.

That was the case with Moses some 13 centuries before Christ. After successfully leading the Israelites out of slavery in Egypt toward freedom in the Promised Land, Moses had problems with a somewhat rebellious and cantankerous group.

So he complained to God, "I am not able to carry all these people alone, the burden is too heavy for me" (Numbers 11:14). In fact, Moses was so discouraged he asked God to kill him unless he helped him.

So God asked Moses to gather 70 men whom he knew to be natural leaders and officers and to bring them to the tent of meeting, where God manifested his presence. God said, "I will come down and talk with you there; and I will take some of the spirit which is upon you and put it upon them; and they shall bear the burden of the people with you, that you may not bear it yourself alone" (Numbers 11:17). So God's spirit did come upon the 70 and Moses had people to whom he could delegate responsibility and leadership.

Thirteen centuries later, Jesus uses the same number — 70 — to recruit men to help him spread the word about the new kingdom of God. If Moses and the 70 elders were developing the Old Israel, Jesus and the 70 were about to develop the New Israel.

But in Jesus' case, the 70 signify something more. If the 12 apostles were originally sent to the lost sheep of the tribe of Israel, the 70 have a broader mission. They are to announce the coming kingdom not only to Jews, but to Samaritans and Gentiles as well, because in his day, it was popularly believed there were 70 nations in the world. Thus, Jesus' 70 disciples symbolized his universal mission to all the nations — Gentiles and Samaritans included. All the outsiders were now invited to be insiders.

Delegation is difficult for gifted, energetic people like Moses and Jesus because they fear no one can do the job quite as well as they. And they probably are right. Yet, without delegation even the most talented and energetic leaders either burn out or wear out or both.

Besides, delegation by gifted, talented, energetic people to other gifted, talented, spirited people has a multiplying effect. Many people are just waiting to be recognized and to be given a chance to use their abilities for a greater cause. Thus, the leader who delegates wisely can multiply his effect exponentially — much like planting an apple seed to yield an apple tree with apples and seeds uncountable.

When Tom Peters wrote his book, *Thriving On Chaos*, he had something like this in mind — that is, allowing for freedom and creativity by loosening control and delegating. It is precisely what a lot of corporations are doing — decentralizing, delegating and allowing more opportunity for creative synergy.

And it is what has to happen in church boards and committees — delegation. When spirit-filled people like Moses' 70 elders are given challenges and responsibilities, marvelous results can take place for the kingdom of God.

Want to get the job done? Follow Jesus' example — delegate.

A second way to get the job done is to *discover — discover new opportunities.*

One of the common mistakes of people, businesses and politicians who fail is in their inability or unwillingness to discover new opportunities. Nearly every marketing success story in the last two centuries has had to do with building the proverbial "better mousetrap" and telling people about it.

Think of it, for centuries people thought travel by horseback and horsedrawn buggy was the way to go until the automobile came along, welcomed at first by derision and skepticism. And if for some the automobile was not fast enough, for others the airplane was a defiance of God's laws. "If God had intended man to fly, he would have given him wings." Some can still remember people who made that statement.

Failure is often associated with the assumption that as things have been, they always shall be. Failure often is the inability to accept the new realities. Think, for example, of the Howard Johnson chain of restaurants and motels. At one time a nationwide leader, they have fallen on bad times because they took their definitions of reality from the past rather than the future.

Families sometimes fail for those reasons. Think how often we pass on bad habits from one generation to the next because we somehow think they are normal. Tragically, children who were physically or sexually abused turn around and physically or sexually abuse their own children. And even perhaps more subtly and tragically, we pass our spiritual and psychological abuse from generation to generation. In other words, rather than discovering new opportunities for new familial patterns and realities, we repeat the old.

Churches do the same thing. If churches succeeded 20 years ago with a certain style and manner and approach, they often wrongly assume they can continue that pattern forever. As a consequence, many mainline American churches are aging and dying and also as a consequence the Roman Catholic Church is experiencing a drastic shortage of priests and nuns.

Jesus faced a similar problem. Many of his contemporaries assumed the kingdom of God consisted in the restoration of a small, but prosperous and powerful Davidic Kingdom. They presumed the promulgation of a Jewish exclusivism started by Ezra and Nehemiah to address a need of the past. They were defining the future by the past.

But Jesus, as always, was the revolutionary. He appointed 70 disciples to go to all people — Samaritans and Gentiles included. His kingdom — God's kingdom — was to be inclusive, not exclusive; universal, not provincial. "The fields are white unto the harvest," he said to the 70.

And if they asked where, he replied to look beyond their own fields, beyond their own backyard, beyond their own past definitions of reality. And that is what he says to the church of today. The fields are white unto harvest. The people are there. And I'm delegating you to discover the new opportunities that are there, to bring them into the kingdom.

Want to get the job done? Then *dedicate* yourself to the task.

You will note that after Jesus pointed out that the fields were white unto the harvest he said to his disciples that they should pray to the Lord of the harvest that he would send forth laborers. The harvest is plentiful, but the laborers are few. Pray, therefore, for dedicated laborers.

Some years ago Russell Conwell wrote a best-selling book titled, *Acres of Diamonds*. He pointed out that the world is full of diamond-like opportunities for those with eyes to see. But one reason people are not dedicated to mining the acres of diamonds is because they cannot see the opportunities. Remember the stories of people in Pennsylvania who were irked at the oil oozing into their fresh water for their cattle — irked that is, until someone discovered what could be done with that oil. Then they were dedicated to harvesting enormous fortunes.

The world, we are told, is full of willing people — some people willing to work, and the rest willing to let them. But the workers are on the side of Jesus and God. "I work," said Jesus, "and my Father in heaven works." If God shuns idleness and laziness, how can we, his people, not be dedicated to his work?

Jesus promised that we would do even greater works than he was doing, if we act in spirit-filled dedication. And just as God gave some of the Divine Spirit to Moses' 70 elders, so has Jesus breathed on his followers the Divine Spirit to be empowered for Divine work.

Most any successful person will tell you that persistence in a task is a major factor in success. Many tell us that success is ten percent inspiration and 90 percent perspiration. It is to be remembered that God is not only the Divine, Creative Mind of the universe. He is also the Divine, Creative Energy of the universe. God not only thinks. He acts. He gets things done.

Jesus asked his disciples to pray for laborers to help reap the fields white unto harvest. And we may well imagine that when these dedicated, praying people finished their prayers, it dawned on them that they should volunteer to be one of the laborers, one of those delegated to discover new opportunities for the success God is wishing to give them. Because God, of all people, wants his kingdom to grow, to succeed, to become more and more universal and inclusive.

However, there is a word of warning to dedicated people, because dedicated people can sometimes be foolish and wasteful in their determination. You will notice that Jesus told the 70 that if people don't receive them and their message, shake the dust off their feet as judgment against them, and move on to the next new opportunity.

As the old saying has it: "If the horse is dead, get off." If people don't respond to the gospel, move on to those who do. If people after repeated invitations refuse to return to church, move on to those open and receptive to the gospel. "If the horse is dead, get off."

If they won't receive you, shake the dust off your feet and move on. If the territory is overworked, if that market is saturated, for heaven's sake, move on.

Want to get the job done? Most all of us do. And Jesus, our Lord and Master teacher, shows us how — delegate, discover, and dedicate yourself to the enormous tasks at hand. Jesus and politicians do have a lot in common, except that Jesus delivered on his promises. He promised, "I will build my church and the gates of hell will not prevail against it." And the promise came true — a church a billion strong and growing — growing throughout the world.

The fields are indeed white unto the harvest. Pray that the Lord will send us many dedicated laborers to go out and to bring in the harvest.

Ordinary Time 15
Luke 10:25-37

The Persistent Noise Of Solemn Assemblies

There is hardly a better-known or better-loved story in the New Testament than that of the Good Samaritan. A Jewish scholar says that it "is one of the simplest and noblest among the noble gallery of parables in the Synoptic Gospels. Love, it tells us, must know no limits of race .... Who needs me is my neighbor. Whom at the given time and place I can help with my active love, he is my neighbor and I am his."[1] So it is that Jesus illustrates in an unforgettable way what it means to be neighborly.

However, the story of the Good Samaritan has been variously interpreted through the centuries. Saint Augustine, for example, in the fifth century, attached varieties of allegorical meanings to it. The fallen man was Adam. Jerusalem represented heaven, the thieves were the devil and his angels, and so on. Therefore, since such an auspicious figure as Augustine has tampered with the parable, I thought we might take a little liberty with it, to make its meaning as lucid as possible. Here is one way we might translate it.

Behold, a white, middle-class Protestant deacon was going through an inner city neighborhood, when he was attacked and robbed by some drug addicts who left him half dead. Now a black minister happened by on his way home from church, but didn't want to get involved, and didn't want to be accused of being an Uncle Tom, and pretended he didn't see. And a black soloist came by, but he was already late for his church service, his solemn assembly, so he couldn't, in good conscience, keep the people waiting at the church any longer, and he hesitated, but then went on.

But it so happened that a black militant came by, saw the white, middle-class deacon, sprayed antiseptic and put band-aids on his wounds, loaded him into his car, took him to the hospital, and paid for his room for two days in advance, inasmuch as the black militant did not know that the white, middle-class Protestant deacon had Blue Cross-Blue Shield, and three company health and hospitalization policies.

Now, who, in this case, was the neighbor, and who was being neighborly?

Or consider another translation.

Behold, a certain black middle-class deacon went through a predominantly white neighborhood and fell among some hoodlums who robbed him and beat him and left him half dead in the gutter.

Now by chance, a very well-dressed Republican businessman passed by on his way to Rotary, a most solemn assembly, where a speech on humanitarian betterment was to be heard. He already was late, already in danger of not fulfilling his attendance quota. So he really couldn't risk stopping, and pretended not to notice.

So likewise, a little less well-dressed Democrat passed by on his way to the Lion's meeting, a slightly less-solemn assembly, where he was to be the tail-twister. Since this was his first time in that honorable position, and since he already was late, he felt he could not stop. He did, however, give a moment's serious consideration to calling Washington to see if there might be something they could do to help this poor fellow. But alas, he was without telephone change.

But after that, there journeyed by a blue-collar Independent, Polish factory worker from Cicero, Illinois, on his way to the tavern. And seeing the beaten, wounded, black, middle-class Protestant deacon in the gutter, he stopped his car, administered first-aid, called the ambulance and the police, followed them to the hospital, where the blue-collar, Independent, Polish factory worker paid for the black, middle-class deacon's room and care in advance.

Now, who was the neighbor and who was being neighborly?

By this famous story, *Jesus made an inclusive critique of the religion of his time.* Like ours, the religion of his time had affirmed regularly that the two greatest commandments were to love God with all your heart, mind, soul and strength and your neighbor as yourself. And it was the priest who should have known that truth most of all, for he represented not only religious leadership of his people, but the economic and political aristocracy as well.

The same was true of the Levite, since he was of the same priestly, aristocratic class, with responsibilities for the music in temple worship. Priest and Levite supposedly represented the best Israel had to offer in religion and culture, but that, said Jesus, was not enough, because there was no true love for the fellow man in need.

A few years ago Peter Berger, a sociologist and Lutheran lay theologian, wrote a book called *The Noise of Solemn Assemblies.* He took his title from the ancient prophet of Amos where he says of the religious people of 750 B.C.:

> *I hate, I despise your feasts,*
> *and I take no delight in your*
> *solemn assemblies.*

Amos went on to say:

> *Even though you offer me your burnt offerings*
> *and cereal offerings, I will not accept them,*
> *And the peace offerings of your fatted beasts*
> *I will not look upon.*
> *Take away from me the noise of your songs;*
> *to the melody of your harps I will not listen.*

And then Amos concludes his critique of their religious services by saying in his majestic, now famous, words:

> But let justice roll down like waters,
> and righteousness like an everflowing stream.
>
> *(Amos 5:21-24)*

Peter Berger wrote in the spirit of an Amos, saying that many churches had become preoccupied with the noise of their solemn assemblies, their religious services. They went through all the religious words and ceremonies, but failed to see the implications of those very words for their relationship to their fellow-man. They knew the hymns and scriptures, but were not cognizant of the deep needs of their neighbors. Socially and economically secure, the priest and Levite, in Jesus' time and ours, believed they had a balanced perspective and good religious behavior. Yet the point of Amos', and Jesus', and Berger's critique is that quite the opposite is true. In the Jewish and Christian faiths, love for God must be followed by love for neighbor — a dimension that has been lacking in many of the priests and Levites of every generation.

And alas, ironically, it is the noise of our solemn assemblies that often clouds the issue. And by solemn assemblies I now mean, not only the assemblies of the church, but as well the assemblies of the Democratic and Republican parties, academic and social reformers, students and other dissenting and protesting and rights groups. Often we fall into the error of thinking that talking about neighbor-love is the same thing as actual neighbor-love. Too frequently the passing of resolutions substitutes for real social change, and florid rhetoric replaces concrete, constructive action. There is a persistent noise in our solemn assemblies that distracts our attention and energies from the genuine human need and suffering of the people around us. But in Jesus' story, it is ironically, the despised, shunned, religiously questionable Samaritan who, in fact, demonstrated the love of God.

All this is not to say that interior religion and solemn assemblies are unimportant. However, if in the Christian faith, we begin within — within the deep reaches of the personality, the soul, the spirit — in the dimension of commitment and devotion and prayer — if we *begin* within these areas, we cannot stop there. If the first movement of the spirit is inward, the second movement must be outward. People of an automobile culture know that it's a fundamental law of life that if there is intake there must be exhaust. If you inhale, you must exhale.

It is no less true in the spiritual realm as far as Christianity is concerned. If you take in, you've got to give out. If you inhale the spirit of God, you've got to exhale it as well. Yet strange as it may seem, many Christians seem to ignore that truth.

It is interesting to note that the Greek word in the Bible for Spirit is *pneuma*, which means, not only spirit, but wind or breath. Thus we have pneumatic tires — tires full of pneuma or wind, and we have pneumonia, a disease of the body's wind apparatus. Thus the Spirit of God is, as it were, the wind or breath of God. So it is that in the Genesis creation story, God breathes his breath or Spirit into Adam and Adam becomes a living soul. Likewise today, a person full of life and breath and spirit is said to be inspired — and in-spirited.

Most churches agree that we ought to make it our business to inspire, to encourage, to strengthen, to give peace and help to those who need it. People come to church expecting to be filled and renewed and refreshed. And that is a proper expectation, one that all churches should try to fulfill.

Yet many churches carry that to the extreme wherein they become all intake and no exhaust. And the simplest of automobile mechanics can tell you that all intake and no exhaust means an early death of an engine. And the simplest of armchair amateur psychologists can tell you that all taking and no giving spells the quick psychological demise and death of a person. And so too with organizations and institutions. When they begin to turn in on themselves, forgetting the people they were established to help, they became stagnant like a backwater slough that has no outlet.

If bureaucracies can turn in on themselves, spending most of their energies making their own internal wheels turn, so can churches. They can be like the machine I once saw featured in a Sunday paper. It had hundreds of wheels, pulleys, belts, levers, buttons and flashing lights. But when the builder was asked what the machine actually did, what sort of work it accomplished, he replied, saying, "Oh nothing. It just sits there and spins and spins within itself." So too with many do-gooder organizations. So too with many churches. This is not to say that the church has no important functions within itself. It most surely has. But it is to say that this is not the only function the church has. Outreach must be an increasingly important activity as well as inreach. Exhaust as well as intake. Nor can we sit idling our engine in neutral all the time. We have to put this huge power plant of a church in gear so as to accomplish the work we are called to do.

We do believe that it is the Spirit of God working with our spirits which empowers us for the work he has in the world. But there are various ways of using his spirit. One way is to draw it in like a huge balloon or blimp and then just sort of float around. Initially we can take in a rather huge volume, but otherwise our intake volume is quite limited. We can be full of only so much wind or spirit.

I believe the church is called to be more of a jet plane than a blimp. Jet planes are trim and sleek, and while at first glance may not appear to take in as much air as blimps, at second glance are known to take in enormous quantities of air, mix it with fuel, and then exhaust it to propel the plane all over the world. We are called to do that — to take in enormous quantities of the Spirit of God, mix it with the fuel of our energy and intelligence and love, and then exhaust it to propel the church on its mission and ministry of social justice and love in its community.

Many churches float around like pious blimps with the appearance of being full of the spirit, when they may be only full of hot air! But a jet plane church for the jet age can fool no one. Because it is designed for work and service it must have huge intake *and* exhaust or it will fall. We are, I believe, being challenged by God to be a jet church for a jet age, a people concerned not only for the intake of the spirit, but for its outflow to others as well.

But we are called upon to take the spirit of God into the world. *We are asked to be bearers of his truth as well.*

Religious people in general, and Christians in particular, often have been seekers after the truth. And since the Renaissance and Enlightenment, men of science and letters have regarded themselves as great, and fearless seekers after truth.

However, Christians often find themselves differing with others, because they speak of having found the truth in Jesus, whom they call the Christ. Now, what do they mean — that they have found the truth about chemistry or physics or atomic energy in Jesus? Hardly that! Do they mean that in Jesus they have discovered all the truth of the world and universe, that Jesus is some sort of highly compressed, miniaturized computer from which answers to all questions issue forth? Surely not that.

No, Christians mean, it seems to me, that in Jesus they have seen the truth about the nature of man and the nature of God. It is not that they believe that by looking at Jesus one enters into a static and suspended state of truth. Not that. For Jesus and his disciples thought not of God or Truth in that way. God, for them, was truth and truth was God. But more than that, God was active truth, not static truth. He was not just being, sitting there in his divine essence. He was not just noun, but verb; not just meditation, but production; not just reflection, but action.

Thus the command to love the Lord thy God with all thy heart and mind, or emotions and intellect, was one that required inward commitment and resolve. But the rest of the commandment requiring love with soul and strength, or will and energy, implied action. Likewise with the second great commandment of love thy neighbor. It involves action — action of justice and love.

As one scholar put it: "God was true. And God demanded that his servants should be like Him. To know the truth, therefore, is to stand under the imperative of God, and so the object of knowledge has become the subject of action."[2] So it is that God says, "Be ye holy as I am holy." Knowing the truth means not only contemplating it, but doing it. Believing in God's justice and love means manifesting it in the world. Worship of God and Jesus as Lord implies practical service to fellow man in organizations and structures of justice and love as well as personal participation.

Jesus saw that, and by his faithfulness to the truth of God, that is, God's intention for a true mankind, he became the Truth, the True Man, the one who was faithful to the will of God right up to and including his own death. In his own action he embodied the action of God. In his own will he embodied the will of God, and thus became the manifestation of God's will. Acknowledging God as his Father, he became a true Son of God, succeeding where Adam had failed. Thus we call him Lord, meaning "noble man," for we regard him as just that — history's first and greatest noble man, not because of genealogy, but because of his faithfulness to the truth, to the activity of God, which is love.

Therefore, if we are to be followers of Jesus, whom we call our Lord, we shall have to take seriously not only the first commandment to love the Lord our God with all our heart, soul, mind and strength, but also the commandment to love our neighbor as ourselves. And that is not easy, especially in our day of strident voices of fragmentation. But love we must if we are at all to catch the vision of Jesus; and love we must, if we are to help our suffering, starving, dying neighbors; love we must if we are to keep the seething hatred and violence of the world from erupting into an end-all conflagration on this old powder-keg earth. Indeed, many scientists and ecologists are now saying that the only possible way to survive is to begin to take seriously the teachings of Jesus as set forth in the Sermon on the Mount.

Consequently, far too many churches are engrossed in the persistent noise of solemn assemblies, telling themselves how much they love God while ignoring their fellow-man. Many groups celebrate their great faith in God, but show little evidence of follow-through in service of God, which is to love our neighbor. Many do-gooder and reform organizations clamor piously, yet noisily, in their solemn assemblies about all the good that ought to be done, while they themselves are imperialist and dogmatic and myopically unloving in their demands.

So it is that most anyone can make noise. But to make music, to effect harmony and balance requires patient, persistent love. It is relatively easy to raise strident voices in clamoring protest, but significantly difficult to carry through with regular and meaningful reform. Therefore, let the persistent noise of the solemn assemblies of various reform groups not be a smoke screen for real reformation. But let it not be that for the church either, knowing that we shall receive the greater judgment.

We are called for involvement, for participation in the world. We are called for reform, for new visions of social structuring, for generous and sympathetic aid for the weak and suffering. Christianity is not a religion for the survival of the fittest, or the richest, or the privileged, or the most brutal. It is a religion for the survival of the weak as well as the strong, the poor as well as the wealthy, the sick as well as the healthy. It is a religion for the survival, not only of the self, but of the brother. It is a religion whose posture is always that of loving the neighbor — that human being or groups of human beings, whoever they are or wherever they might be, who are in need of what we can give them or get for them.

The persistent noise of solemn assemblies is that noise which keeps saying, "We believe," and "We love," but does nothing to help our fellow man. As the Letter of James in the New Testament puts it, "My brothers, what use is it for a man to say he has faith when he does nothing to show it? Can that faith save him? Suppose a brother or a sister is in rags with not enough food for the day, and one of you says, 'Good luck to you, keep yourselves warm, and have plenty to eat,' but does nothing to supply their bodily needs. What is the good of that? So with faith, if it does not lead to action, it is in itself a lifeless thing" (James 2:14-17, NEB). Let this judgment fall not only upon the church, which it most surely does, but upon all noisy solemn assemblies. Love and faith must be manifested in action toward fellow man.

In the third place, *we are called upon to manifest spirit and truth corporately as well as individually.*

We could, of course, speak of many modern variations of the Good Samaritan story. We could have some medical doctors pass by on the other side, unwilling to stop out of fear for later being sued for malpractice. We could have certain law and order advocates who want order at any price, who pass by on the other side in pursuit of the robbers, ignoring the victim's cry for help.

Far more often however, those of us accustomed to solemn assemblies have taken the role of the pious individualist who helps the victim but ignores the larger social factors that led to the crime in the first place. For example, the road from Jerusalem to Jericho had a notorious reputation, and was at one time called the "Ascent of Blood" (since it was a 3,400-foot ascent into Jerusalem). In the fourth century Jerome said the road was still full of brigands and robbers. And in the 19th century a certain professor, Hackett, visited the Jericho Road and observed that even yet it abounded with thieves and robbers.

We believe that Jesus was not by this story intending to illustrate that only individualistic neighbor-love was acceptable. Without a doubt he pressed the case for the true expression of individual neighbor-love. But he did not stop there, nor should we. The responsible self, the involved Christian, will be concerned not only to help the victim, but to improve the Jericho Road as well. He will want to remove the hiding places, install more lights, increase police patrol and then search out ways to reform the criminal, investigating the social and economic factors leading to the crime.

Nor are we to believe Jesus would tolerate those who play injured and sick, milking the tender-hearted of their money. Jesus' demand for justice and his understanding of love would not allow that. He calls us all to be responsible selves. And once the victim is well he is expected to leave the sick room to perform responsibly in society, not to live parasitically.

Paul, in his letter to the Galatians, saw that we all fall victim to weakness and failure, and said, "Bear one another's burdens, and so fulfill the law of Christ" (Galatians 6:2). And in his letter to the Romans he wrote, "We that are strong ought to bear the infirmities of the weak, and not to please ourselves" (Romans 15:1). The law of the jungle where only the strongest or fittest or most brutal survive has no place in the Christian faith, where the strong, instead of exploiting and destroying the weak, are to help them. But lest the weak turn that truth to their advantage wherein they are exploiting the strong, mooching off their generosity, greedily drinking in the milk of human kindness, let it be remembered that Paul advised that when they regain their strength, "each man will have to bear his own load" (Galatians 6:5). We all belong to the family of man and must be responsible to each other in that relationship.

In conclusion, let us say that the noise of all sorts of solemn assemblies is very persistent today. Sentimental romanticists, naive utopians and vicious revolutionary anarchists abound. But let those of us in the church not be deluded by ideologies which do not deal with the pride and selfishness of human beings. But on the other hand, let us not be withdrawn and lulled to sleep by the pious, individualistic ethic that has no concern for the society at large. Let us overcome the noise to make the music of harmonious human relationships of justice and love.

There is one final aspect of the Good Samaritan story that often goes unnoticed — it is the reaction of the Good Samaritan's wife when he got home and she found out that the money he spent to help the victim who was mugged, was the money she was going to use to buy new drapes. Without giving him much time to explain what happened to the money, she exclaimed, "Oh, you lousy Samaritan, you've spent my money again on something that shouldn't concern you. You're going to get yourself in trouble some day, helping all those people along the way. Leave them alone. Their trouble is none of your business. Don't get involved."

Alas, poor good Samaritan, enduring the pious noise of yet another solemn assembly in his home. But he responded to the ancient question God put to Cain centuries earlier, saying quietly, "But, I am my brother's keeper."

So are we.

---

1. Montefiore. *The Synoptic Gospels,* II (London: Macmillan and Co., 1909), p. 468.

2. Hoskyns and Davey. *The Riddle Of The New Testament,* (London: Faber and Faber, Limited, 1958), p. 29.

Troubled Journey

John G. Lynch

Foreword

Many times in life we find ourselves in the midst of a troubled journey. Often, the trouble is intensely personal, even spiritual, in nature. At such points, we need a guide, someone rooted in the solid reality of God's Word. As these meditations show, Pastor John G. Lynch is such a guide.

Pastor Lynch has experienced the troubled journey himself. And he shares with us what he learned — that the answers to our dilemmas are found in the story of God's loving, faithful relationship with his people.

John G. Lynch has been my friend and pastor for many years. But above all he has been a guide. A guide to the rich, nurturing, yet challenging, Word of God. And in God's Word I have found direction during my troubled journeys.

I truly hope that you, the reader, will discover in these meditations God's plan for you — the path through a troubled journey to that peace of God which surpasses all understanding.

                    Michael J. Kurtz, Ph.D.
                    President, Lutheran Historical Society
                    Gettysburg
                    July 1993

Introduction

Many years ago I spent two glorious weeks at a study and work camp near Taizé, France. Twenty-five men and women from 16 nations studied the Bible and Third World concerns each morning and worked together building a retreat house each afternoon. On our last day we took a pilgrimage from Taizé to Macon, where the famous vineyards grow. This was no ordinary pilgrimage. We walked separately in silence each five kilometer stretch, the person ahead just barely in view. Every fifth kilometer we gathered together to share thoughts from our solitary walks. In that rolling, peaceful land, troubled thoughts arose. We had grown close to each other in those two weeks. Most of us would never see each other again. We had overcome language barriers, racial differences, conflicting social customs. Prayer at Taizé was powerful in those days, as we pressed together in that grand church bathed in the evening sun's rays. I have rarely had a more powerful experience of prayer. Taizé nourished my passion for God's Word as few places have.

The meditations in this book center on Jesus' long and troubled journey to Jerusalem. Luke tells us that Jesus, "when the days drew near for him to be received up, set his face to go to Jerusalem." Early on in that journey, he stopped to visit Mary and Martha. This book begins in their home. We all have our own journeys to Jerusalem. My hope and prayer for you is that these meditations will lead you anew to God's Word, that great lamp unto our feet on our troubled journeys.

I have a special word of reverence and thanks for all who helped me in the preparation of this book, especially Diana Mathis, who typed the manuscripts with such great care; Dr. Michael Kurtz, for his encouraging words of Foreword; and Kenne Miller, my Katie von Bora, whose incisive editing has vastly improved the quality of this book.

Ordinary Time 16
Luke 10:38-42

The Better Part

During World War II the Royal Air Force flew Danny's favorite plane of all time: the Spitfire. Watching those things fly all over the RKO newsreels the young boy came to believe they were dauntless. If a pilot flew a Spitfire, Danny thought, he would always hit his target, and he would always return home.

One day the British Consul from Minneapolis came to Danny's town to visit. Danny's dad was chairman of the County War Bond drive so that gave him the honor of entertaining the British Consul in his home. His mother, Suzanne, went crazy with preparations. She brought in all her friends; she hired a German woman to clean the house; she went downtown to buy a new dress.

The day the Consul arrived 40 people crammed into three rooms to welcome this man. Each one of those people couldn't wait to tell this tall, thin diplomat from England about the town, about how patriotic it was, about how he or she had a great-aunt in London, about how well the war was going. They all had plenty to say.

Suzanne was running around fractiously trying to serve everybody and greet everybody, and make sure everybody had a place to sit, and did they want more of this — in general, were they having a good time.

Finally the British Consul sat down. For a split second he was actually by himself. The hostess had left to get him a drink; all the other guests momentarily turned away. Danny saw his chance. He ran to him. Even though the Consul was sitting, the boy still had to stand to whisper into his ear: "Tell me about Spitfires!"

The tall man looked at the eight-year-old. He smiled, he relaxed, and he said, "Spitfires? I'll tell you a story about Spitfires. I flew one early in the war. It was splendid. I shot down a Messerschmidt and I came home alive. The next time I wasn't so lucky. That's why I'm not flying anymore. What is your name? I'll send you some pictures of Spitfires."

About a month later a letter came from Minneapolis. Inside was a folder about Spitfires and a note from the Consul: "Dear Danny. I enjoyed talking with you. Good luck." He signed his name.

Danny was the only person who didn't barrage the Consul's ears with information about the town and American patriotism. This small boy was the only one who said, "Tell me about Spitfires." He was the only one who actually listened to him — even if it was just for a few minutes!

In this passage from Luke's gospel Jesus needs somebody to listen. He has just begun his journey to Jerusalem where he knows he will go through the bitter road of cross and denial and abandonment and betrayal to the glory of resurrected life.

As he began his journey he entered a Samaritan village where the villagers said: "You can stay here." His disciples wanted to burn the village to the ground. Jesus had to tell them, "No, you don't know what stuff you are made of when you want to do things like that."

Another man came to him to ask: "I will follow you, but first let me go and say farewell to those back home." Jesus replied: "No one who puts his hand to the plow and looks back is fit for the kingdom of God."

Then he sent out his 72 disciples to teach and to heal the sick. When they came back they said, "Even the demons are subject to us in your name!" Jesus shook his head again.

They were all missing the point. "Don't rejoice that the spirits are subject to you," he said. "Rejoice that your names are written in heaven."

Then a scribe asked him what he had to do to inherit eternal life. Jesus said, "Love the Lord your God, love your neighbor, and love yourself." The scribe, seeking to justify himself, went on, "And who is my neighbor?"

Jesus, exasperated, finally crawled into the home of his good friends, Mary and Martha. He plopped down on a bench, shaking his head. "They are all missing it," he said. Martha ran into the kitchen to get him something to drink. He didn't even notice her go. Mary sat at his feet and listened. "They are all missing it," he went on. "My disciples want to burn villages to the ground. Some want to go home for three months to say good-bye to everybody before they do anything. They will never get started." Mary kept on listening.

"I told this scribe, who wanted to do something to inherit eternal life, to say his prayer every day: 'Love the Lord your God with your whole mind and soul and strength,' and then I told him, 'Love your neighbor as yourself.' Do you know what he said? 'And who is my neighbor?' So I told him the story of the Good Samaritan but I don't think he got it.

"So I wonder where this mission is going." Mary kept on listening. She listened because she believed that in listening to Jesus she would hear the Word of God reaching to her and calling to her. In listening to whatever he had to say she would grow as his word planted itself in her heart. They would grow together: one speaker with one listener.

Then out of the kitchen came Martha. "Lord," she hollered. "Don't you care that my sister has left me to serve alone? Tell her to get up and help me!" Martha had heard nothing that Jesus had to say. She kept imposing her own agenda on the Lord. She couldn't let things be; she couldn't let things cool down. That's what Jesus needed to do. She had to stir up a lot of bustle in the kitchen, a lot of distracting concerns, so she didn't have to listen to what was really going on in Jesus' heart or in her own.

Jesus answered her: "Martha, Martha, you are anxious and troubled about many things. You need to listen for a while. For a long while. You need to let things cool down in your life. Too many cares are distracting you. Only one thing is needful, and Mary has chosen that good part."

The next verse in Luke's gospel reads this way: "He was praying in a certain place ..." Actually he was praying out loud when Mary sat at his feet. She was listening to his prayer. Jesus spoke to God about everything. Sometimes alone. Sometimes with people like Mary around to hear him. Poor Martha. She missed it. She had too many concerns and distractions.

Later on a woman in the crowd cried out to Jesus: "Blessed the womb that bore thee and the breasts that nursed thee." Jesus cried back: "Rather, blessed are those who hear the Word of God and keep it."

Martin Luther said that those who listen are those who are truly wise, because they always begin anew so that they may forget the things that are behind and stretch themselves to what is ahead. But the lukewarm and the hypocrites, he said, think they have already chosen what is best. "They forget what is before them and fall back into what is behind them, and there they rest and snore."[1]

Good listeners. That's what Jesus gifts us to be. As good listeners we press forward and forget the things that are behind. We reach out, with our ears open, to what God is calling us to be in the future. He will speak to us in many persons and in many ways. He will bring new voices to sing with us and to speak with us, and we will grow as we listen.

He will speak to us in the Bible; he will speak to us in those whom we love and who love us. Sometimes he will speak to us, too, in the voices of our adversaries.

One thing is needful — to sit at the feet of Jesus and hear his Word daily. This is the best part to choose and it shall not be taken away.

---

1. *Luther's Works,* 11, (Concordia, 1976), p. 541-542.

Ordinary Time 17
Luke 11:1-13

When Did Jesus Pray?

Jesus, at those critical times when he had momentous decisions to make, withdrew to the hills to pray. In the sixth chapter of Luke's gospel, when he had healed that man's withered hand in the synagogue on the sabbath, he threw the gauntlet at the rules and regulations that for so long had choked out the kingdom of God. To the scribes and the Pharisees he offered this challenging question: "I ask you, is it lawful on the sabbath to do good or to do harm, to save life or to destroy it?" Luke tells us these scribes and Pharisees were filled with fury (the word actually means madness). They lost their good sense as they discussed with one another what they might do to Jesus.

Before he made his next move, Jesus withdrew from those scribes and Pharisees with their unbridled, senseless anger and went to the hills to pray. The New Testament word for prayer means to assert our rights before God. The gospels also teach that as creatures we have only one right before God ... our constant and thirsting need for his sovereignty in our lives.

Away for a while in prayer he made his decision. God's sovereignty re-established in his life, he did not go back to the synagogue to tell those scribes and Pharisees where to get off. He did not return for full scale battle in their arena. No, when it was day, directly but quietly he called his disciples and chose from them 12 whom he named apostles: those whom he would send out before him to the places where he himself was to go. It is good strategy to call those loyal to your side when you sense you are under attack. Prayer gave Jesus the courage to do this.

Later, in the ninth chapter of his gospel, Luke tells of another critical prayer time in Jesus' life. King Herod, hearing all that Jesus had done, wanted to know just who this carpenter's son from Nazareth thought he was. He sought to see him. Jesus knew that meant trouble, for Herod had a multitude of motives and a train load of ruthless reasons why he wanted to see Jesus. When they finally did meet, shortly before Pilate put Jesus on the cross, Herod wanted Jesus to work a miracle for him, which Jesus refused to do. So Herod treated him with contempt and mockery and sent him back to Pontius Pilate. Hearing that Herod wanted to see him, Jesus once again withdrew to prayer alone with God, asserting once again his need for God's sovereignty in his life.

After his prayer, Jesus did not go to Herod and say, "Well, here I am. Let me tell you more about myself." No, he stuck to those loyal to him. He told *them* more about himself, his mission, his destiny, and what was in store for them. "I will suffer many things. I will be rejected by the scribes and elders. I will be killed. But on the third day I will be raised." The lesson from this prayer? "Wait for that third day!"

Then, as he moved toward Jerusalem with his 12 loyal disciples and at least 70 others, too, success came. They healed and cast out demons. God's kingdom began to break into people's lives as it never had before. Yet success has its problems, too. Success makes some people uneasy; it makes others jealous; it makes others resentful. So now those successful, loyal followers of Jesus needed help. They needed God's sovereignty in their lives more than ever.

Once again he went to pray. This time, when he finished his prayer, he did not choose his loyal friends. That was already done. He did not clarify for them what the future would hold. That, too, he had already done. Now he had to give them something to hang onto once he was gone. It was not a badge, a uniform, a slogan, a picture, or a statue. He gave them something to encourage them to move forward with hope and honor and success. He gave them a prayer: the prayer of God's sovereignty in our lives.

"Father, hallowed be thy name." God is father, above and beyond what his creatures are, not subject to their hatreds and jealousies and their discomfort with success.

"Thy kingdom come." Thy kingdom — that's wherever you act on our behalf, wherever your light burns out our darkness, wherever your hope destroys our despair, wherever your faith enables us to believe in a future and leave behind our fear and terror of success.

"Give us each day our daily bread." Whatever we need to nourish our faith, hope, love, and our talents to serve you. Father in heaven, give us that.

"And forgive us our sins." Because you have first forgiven us, we let our grudges go and forgive those who impede us ... we let them go.

"And lead us not into temptation." Luther says about this part of the Lord's Prayer that no one can escape temptations and allurements so long as we live in the flesh and have the devil prowling about us. But we pray here that we may not fall into them and be overwhelmed by them.

Many times tribulations and entanglements arise in congregations. They come for a multitude of reasons and a multitude of purposes. This passage from Luke gives us a clue as how best to deal with them. Church members can vote in meetings; they can argue procedures; they can discuss in forums. This is all helpful. But Martin Luther said, as he ended this part of his commentary on the Lord's Prayer, that at such times of distress our only help or comfort is to take refuge in the Lord's Prayer and appeal to God from our hearts. If we attempt to help ourselves by our own thoughts and counsels we will only make matters worse.

A congregation's hope for peace and unity lies in prayer. The prayer question is this: What decision will most help the advancement of God's kingdom? What decision will most allow God's sovereignty to reign over us and our future? Jesus gives us the key to the kingdom and God when he teaches us to pray.

Luther, when he wrote his great *Babylonian Captivity of the Church,* said that any obstacle can be removed by the faith of the church and the prayer of faith, just as Stephen converted Paul the apostle by this power. The word of God is powerful enough, when uttered, to change even a godless heart.

Yes, God often sleeps with his children at midnight, just longing to be awakened on our behalf. Often he hides behind the door, just longing to open it for us. Ask and you shall receive; seek and you shall find. Knock and it shall be opened unto you.

In that spirit of renewed trust in God as our future, let us give thanks to him and move forward toward a new day.

Ordinary Time 18
Luke 12:13-21

Rich Toward God

The southern California cities of San Diego and Los Angeles are well known for their misty mornings. Each day in Los Angeles, in the Beverly Hills section, the sky is thick with fog. "Don't worry," the natives will tell you, "it will burn off by noon." And sure enough it does. Every morning it is the same thing ... thick, cold fog until 11 or 12:00. Then sunshine for the rest of the day.

In Annapolis, Maryland, on the east coast, it is exhilarating to walk to the end of the Naval Academy campus and there watch the sun break through the haze over the Chesapeake Bay. It's one of God's great miracles that he sends his sun each day to burn off the fog in southern California or break through the early morning haze over the bay.

The predawn beauty of the early morning is rarely appreciated for its ability to seduce and yet obscure perceptions. The quality of light in that hour is amazing. A murky sort of light, it blends in with the early morning haze and the mist from the face of the earth. Nothing is very clear in that hour before dawn. Trees look like giant ghosts. A man walking in the distance looks like a walking tree. Each thing's identity is confused and bewildering.

The Scandinavians call that hour before dawn the hour of the wolf. In their folklore this is the hour when most men die and most men are born.

That hour appears in our gospel when Jesus says to the young man who wants to force his brother to divide the inheritance, "Life does not consist in the abundance of possessions." That word "possessions" refers to that hour before dawn: that murky, foggy twilight time. In Jesus' mind this man uses his possessions in a murky, foggy, twilight kind of way.

Who is this young man? And what does he want from his brother? This is a younger brother who wants to separate off his share of the inheritance so he can be independent. The problem is that it was never a 50-50 split in those days. The elder brother got at least two-thirds and the younger, at most, one-third of the inheritance. So what this young man wanted to do was take just enough land from his brother to aggravate him and retain just enough for himself that he could barely make a living. He would have been better off to work the land in union with his brother. That's why Psalm 133 prays, "Behold, how good and pleasant it is when brothers dwell in unity." But this younger man, so consumed by a desire to aggravate his older brother, won't do that. "Give me one-third," he says. His brother says, "No way." Then he goes to Jesus to say, "Make him give me enough that I can barely live on. Make him cooperate with my desire to aggravate him."

That's why Jesus says in response, "Man, you are trying to make me a judge and that is not my relationship to you or your brother. This is predawn stuff on your part. Your vision is murky and your desires are still in the fog of the hour of the wolf. I will not be part of your desire to aggravate your brother or your intention to self-destruct. Life does not consist in the abundance of predawn shadow dances."

Later on in this same chapter of Luke's gospel, Jesus will say, "I have a fire to cast over the earth, and how I long that it be enkindled." That fire, in Jesus' mind, is the Word of God: the Word of God burning off the early morning haze in our decisions toward one another, a ball of fire chasing away the fog of early morn lest we allow ourselves to linger in the shadows of petty quarrels and cloaked in self-destruction.

Those glossy picture magazines are handy and entertaining to read while standing in line in a supermarket or waiting for a free chair at the hairdresser. Often these publications will feature articles on entertainment personalities with an opportunity for readers to correspond with their favorite star. One comedian received a letter from a young man named Jeff. Jeff wrote, "My name is Jeff and I'm 12 years old. I got two crummy sisters, aged eight and four. Well, bye for now. Signed Jeff." That boy was not in the twilight zone. He did not operate in the mists before dawn or the murky haze over the earth. Everyone who read that letter knew just how he felt about his sisters. No camouflage in Jeff. His life did not consist in the abundance of twilight activities or feelings.

The gospel wants us to be rich toward God. What does that mean? The gospel is not advocating poverty, destitution, annoyance, or aggravation. Human nature is advocate enough of such feelings. The gospel promotes abundance, overflow and motion toward God.

The young boy in our gospel wants to aggravate his brother and sell himself short. That kind of activity leads no one to abundance. No rivers will overflow their banks with this boy. He will have his one-third or less, his brother will have his share diminished and nobody wins. Jesus says he is like a man who spends his whole life tearing down barns instead of letting the river of his life overflow toward God.

So often Christian preachers go haywire when it comes to abundance and overflow. The gospel clearly advocates both, so long as they are both in motion toward God. Human nature, so uncomfortable with abundance, loves to tear down barns. It's a different story when it comes to gathering in the grain. Notice how the man in the story never does gather anything in. He just plans to. Jesus says don't let your life be simply a storehouse of aggravations or a barn filled with self-destructive actions. Let your life be an overflow toward God and abundance in motion toward him.

Martin Luther, when he was about 48 years old, spent some time with a friend, Hans Loser, to get some physical exercise.

During that time Hans took Luther on a hunting trip on his lands. The prize that Luther "bagged" on that excursion was his commentary on Psalm 147. He later wrote to Hans that this was his happiest hunt and grandest game. He also went on to say that he was sharing all of it — 100 percent — with his friend. In this way Luther demonstrates how we can give away God's gifts of grace and mercy and still have all of it left for our own needs.

This kind of magnanimity is what Jesus is talking about in today's gospel: an open-hearted attitude toward abundance and a positive outlook about the goods of the earth, prayer, possessions, psalms and commentaries on the psalms. God does not want us to be stuck in the hour before dawn. He wants us to be rivers overflowing with his goods and gifts, creatures abundant in him. Let us give thanks to God for his grace toward us and the joyous revelation of his richness toward us.

Ordinary Time 19
Luke 12:32-48

Fearful Flock

One of the really fascinating characters in literature is the Count of Monte Cristo, created over a century ago by Alexander Dumas.

What a beginning! Dumas introduces Edmond Dantes, the young sailor about to become captain of his ship and marry the girl of his dreams. Then he unfolds the story of a double-cross, a false accusation and 14 years in the dungeon of the Chateau D'If. Fourteen years of darkness where brightest hope was the old priest, Abee Faria, who told him of treasure — great treasure — buried on the Isle of Monte Cristo.

Escaping through the sea, Dantes travels with smugglers on the Mediterranean Coast until finally he is alone at the mouth of the treasure cave. The closer Dantes came to that treasure the more terrified he felt. His terror was not that the treasure was a fiction, but that it really was there. Dumas observes that it is one of the strange phenomena of human nature that we feel a dread of the daylight more than the darkness. Why? In the light we can be seen, watched, observed.

It is this kind of fear that Jesus has in mind in our gospel when he tells his disciples, "Fear not, little flock, for it is your father's good pleasure to give you the kingdom." These men and women following Jesus are not afraid of the wolf; they are afraid of the pasture! They want to run and scatter to avoid those green pastures beside still waters. They are fearful of what is in their best interests. They are about to run from the kingdom of God.

A few years ago an old man who had been very successful in the power and light business showed his nephew a telegram dated Christmas Eve 1924. Although Bert was in his 80s and 60 years had passed, he still held onto that telegram. With great satisfaction he said to his nephew, "Look at that date, Jack, and look at that name. This was the biggest deal I ever made and I made it on Christmas Eve."

Bert was not afraid of treasure or pasture or the kingdom of God. He used to ascribe all his successful business dealings to the Holy Spirit. Bert's younger brother, Jack's father, was not like that. He was more fearful, less inclined to risk, less inclined to treasure and less inclined to the kingdom of God.

In this passage from Luke, Jesus has been trying to teach his disciples how eager God is to have their lives overflow with his grace and be abundant with his love and concern. "Consider the lilies of the field," he said, "how they neither toil nor spin. Yet I tell you, even Solomon in all his glory was not arrayed like one of these. And do not be anxious for your father knows what you need. So seek in his kingdom and all these things shall be yours as well."

Soren Kierkegaard, the late Danish Lutheran theologian and pastor, wrote that between God and man there is an eternal, essential difference which cannot be allowed to disappear. For Kierkegaard it is God's authority, his sovereignty and absolute claim on us for our allegiance. Such an allegiance is what faith is all about and it makes us, as Luther says, high-spirited, eager and mettlesome in our relationships with one another and with God. Kierkegaard goes on to comment how much we fear God's sovereignty in our lives and how much we fear allegiance. Such allegiance, Kierkegaard felt, is so risky it scares most people to death.

This is why Jesus tells his disciples, "Fear not, little flock ...." He wants them to risk something on their own, something neither the Pharisees nor the Sadducees nor the Zealots would ever risk ... an absolute trust in God. Jesus calls his disciples to an absolute belief in the Father's good pleasure to give them the kingdom they will be gifted with. An absolute loyalty to the God who says, "I want you to have the treasure of my kingdom, pressed down brimming over."

Then Jesus tells them to sell their possessions. That word for possessions is a favorite word in the Gospel of Luke. It means that which is at the origin of things. Possessions refers to the dawn times in a believer's life and to those beginnings that make believers who they are. They are told to sell all that — take it to the marketplace and barter there with other human beings what each has to offer. Share beginnings and dawn times, especially the dawn times of faith.

In sharing on the marketplace of life, believers begin to sense what they really have in common: their common need for God, for faith and for the treasure of the kingdom of God.

No one in the gospels more saddened Jesus than the rich young man who could not barter in the marketplace all God had given him. He had to hold on to it all, for what reason the gospel doesn't say. Like Edmond Dantes, he trembled before the treasure. The rich young man shunned the light of day and crept back to the darkness of his own heart.

God wants us out in his marketplace of life, negotiating and bargaining all we have with all that everyone else has. Jesus wants his disciples ready, like servants with their loins girt and their lamps lit for the journey that his kingdom inspires.

Martin Luther wrote that although there are many ways to seek the kingdom of God, they are all departures from that one way of believing in Christ and practicing and applying the gospel. This way involves growing and being strengthened at heart through preaching, listening, reading, singing and meditating. It means blossoming out in fruits to advance God's kingdom and to lead many other people to it.

The gospel journey of faith leads to the Lord who meets us as we continue to move. He arrives at the second or third watch, girds himself and ministers unto us. Blessed are those servants, watchful and ready for the Lord's gracious kingdom of peace.

Ordinary Time 20
Luke 12:49-53

Fire
Word

Stretching south for hundreds of miles from Glacier National Park lies a majestic mixture of valleys, rushing streams, and gargantuan mountains called the Bob Marshall Wilderness. Backpackers have hiked there for decades looking for elk, grizzlies and golden eagles. Fortunately the grizzlies stay up in the high country, but a golden eagle may be spotted and the elusive wolverine may be tracked.

The Bob Marshall Wilderness hosts some 90,000 packers and hikers each year, most of them in the months of July and August. They must come in either by foot or horseback. No motorized vehicles are allowed. The forests on those rugged mountain slopes are thick with Lodgepole Pine, a tough, hardy tree with cones so thick that only extreme heat can burst forth the seeds. That's where fire comes in. For thousands — oh, millions of years — lightning has cracked the big sky out there down to the forests below. (Often the lightning will hit the Douglas Firs, less rugged than the Lodgepole Pines, and a forest fire will begin.) For years, of course, the United States Forest Service fought furiously to put out these fires. More recently, they have adopted a policy of managed fires. They have learned these fires have a purpose. Without them the seeds of the Lodgepole Pines are never released. Without them much of the underbrush and plant life there does not regenerate. The earth needs a fire cast on it or it will die.

Jesus, speaking to Peter, that blustery, Lodgepole Pine kind of a man, said, "Peter, I have a fire to cast over the earth, and how I am constrained until it be kindled!" What did Jesus mean? He knew that Peter, like all of his disciples, was a wilderness that needed fire or he would die. Peter needed the fire of God's Word to keep his heart from freezing over and to keep the passion of his soul from cooling down.

Peter had left his fishing business on the Sea of Galilee. That was the first time the fire of God's Word had invaded his life. He was growing cool in that job — cool and bored, casting the same nets each day and each night. A man tends to cool down in boredom. So Jesus came along. "Come, follow me," he said. "Come, let the Word of God heat you up, for you are beginning to cool down."

Not long afterwards Peter returned with Jesus to his mother-in-law's house for dinner. She didn't care much for this Nazarene Rabbi. Feeling chilled, she put out the fire on her hearth and went to bed. Jesus came in and touched her — the word in Greek means he lit her flame — and rekindled her heart. Suddenly she was not so hostile to him any more. God's Word had come to her, reassured her, touched her. And she got up, rekindled the hearth in her home and served Jesus a meal.

Once more, as Jesus and his disciples neared Caesarea Philippi, Peter found his faith and loyalty to Jesus growing cold. The opposition from the scribes and the Pharisees had cast a frost on their little band. Jesus knew they were all cooling down. So he spent a night in prayer. Then he asked them, "Who do men say that I am?" Peter, always ready for the lightning to set his forest ablaze, cried out, "Thou art the Christ, the Son of the Living God." Jesus answered, lest Peter be confused about whence that lightning strike came, "Blessed art thou, Simon Bar Jona, for flesh and blood has not revealed this to thee, but my father who is in heaven."

So it is with us all. We all have those cool down moments, those times when the fires of love grow frosty and the ice of boredom replaces the fire of passion. The chill of ambivalence often caps over loyalty and devotion.

This is part of the human condition. It is quite natural to cool down. It is quite natural to have ice form on our loyalties and friendships. But it is quite beyond nature to have a burning need for the word of God.

The prophet Jeremiah had it. To the people of his time, living their cool lies and dreams, Jeremiah called out, "Hear the word of the Lord! 'Let the prophet who has a dream tell the dream, but let him who has my Word speak my word faithfully. What has straw in common with wheat. Is not my Word like a fire?' says the Lord. 'And like a hammer which breaks the rock in pieces?' "

Before Jeremiah, when the prophet Isaiah was lit to action by God, he saw the seraphim come to him with a burning coal, touch his lips and then say, "Who will serve me?" Only after God's fire touched him could Isaiah say, "Here am I, Lord, here am I."

Like the Lodgepole Pine, we all need the fire of God's Word in our lives, or we will grow cold. We will be ice-capped. Our job will cease. Our friendships will cease. Our marriages will cease. Our very lives will cease, because human nature is so prone to the freeze, so susceptible to an ice cap on the heart.

God knows this. That's why he sends his lightning to strike into our lives lest we stop and regenerate no more. Did not God say to his people as he led them out of the icy slavery of Egypt, "For your Lord God is a devouring fire and a jealous God"?

One time Elijah was called to stand in a test of fire with the prophets of Jezebel's God, Baal. Baal's 450 prophets set up their altar with a sacrificial bull. They danced, shouted incantations and even lacerated themselves until the blood flowed. No fire came from heaven to consume their sacrifice. Then Elijah stepped forward, pouring water over everything. He drenched it all and then he prayed. That's all. No wild cries, no limping dances around the altar, no self lacerations. "O Lord, God of Abraham, Isaac and Israel," he prayed, "let it be known this day that thou art God in Israel, and that I am thy servant and that I have done all these things at thy

Word. Answer me, O Lord, answer me, that this people may know that thou, O Lord, art God, and that thou hast turned their hearts back."

The Bible tells us that then the fire of the Lord fell, it consumed the burnt offering, the wood, the stones, the dust, and licked up the water that was in the trench. This was the fire of God's Word.

Nowhere does the fire of God's Word burn off the ice and cause tumult more than in the differences between generations, in the relationships between father and son and mother and daughter. These relationships tend to freeze over into a cool placidity where mother thinks her daughter must be just as she is, or son thinks he must be a carbon copy of dad. Not so, says the gospel. There will not be agreement between mother and daughter or father and son so much as there will be distinction; each will have a proper share of the kingdom of God. God's Word burns off the ice of mutual identification and kindles the fire of proper identity over and over again.

No, it is not peace in the sense of placidity or tranquility that God's Word brings. It is fire: the fire of each person's identity and each person's proper share of the kingdom of God.

Thus, set ablaze by God's Word, we fan the flames for one another and keep God's love burning in our hearts.

Ordinary Time 21
Luke 13:22-30

The Narrow Gate

One long, shadowy afternoon, when the light was more smoke than light, a young American of Russian descent wandered along a canal in Leningrad, searching for the Palace of Prince Yarosof, where the monk Rasputin had been killed. Leningrad in winter is not a cheery place. The sun rises late in the morning and sets about 4 p.m. Daylight, always weak and wintry, never rises above a sinister haze. In that light Alex sought his narrow door.

He didn't realize quite what he was seeking. Only when he found it did he know why he had wandered most of the day in that sinister, smoky light. He thought he was looking for the murderous palace where the princes had poisoned, shot, and finally drowned Rasputin, so immune to their murderous ways. But God had a new discovery in store for him. God was leading Alex to his wide path.

The young American found the palace, a small, stylish structure recently used by the communists as an office for some department of the Proletariat. He wandered through the grounds, peeking through this portico, squinting into that dark corner, trying to find the key to why they had murdered the notorious Rasputin here: trying to catch the flavor of the place the way it was when they had killed him.

That's when he found God's wide path over a small portico on the palace grounds. He saw written in a familiar alphabet these Latin words, "Deus Omnia Conservat" — "God takes care of everything." What a surprise! What a secret to discover in a Bolshevik palace the word "Deus" etched boldly in stone declaring that God takes care of everything ... Rasputin, the princes who killed him, the Russian people, and even an American wandering in that half-lit city.

When Alex found the narrow gate, it wasn't narrow after all. He had hoped to find, by diligent inquiry, some clue to those turbulent times in Russian history. By careful scrutiny he had planned to unearth for himself the treasure that would tell him all. He looked for something suspicious and evil — an omen that he could claim his own. Instead God led him to a simple, fundamental truth about himself — a truth as broad as the Steppes of Siberia, a truth as wide as the world: "Deus Omnia Conservat." "God takes care of everything."

The Pharisees in Jesus' day were specialists of the narrow gate. They really promoted narrow gate living, preaching the 613 prescriptions of the Mosaic Law as the answer to all life's problems. "Hold fast to these," they said, "and then God will love you." They did not have the faintest notion that God takes care of everything, the 613 prescriptions notwithstanding.

Shortly before Jesus told this young man about the narrow gate, a woman had walked into the synagogue on the sabbath day. For 18 years she had a spirit of infirmity. Bent over, she could not straighten herself out. When Jesus saw her he called her and said, "Woman, thou art freed from your infirmity." He laid his hands upon her. Immediately she was straightened out and she praised God.

What did the ruler of the synagogue do? He was indignant because Jesus had done this on the sabbath. For centuries leaders of synagogues had been telling people, "You come to God only by the narrow door of the sabbath and its laws." Little did they know that God has no need of that narrow gate, or of any other narrow gate humankind can construct to control access to the healing power of God. His mercy is as wide as the Steppes of Siberia, as vast as the world. It knows no limits. It has no narrow gate!

This ruler of the synagogue was so indignant that he said to the woman and to all the people standing around, "There are six days on which work ought to be done. Come on those days to be healed and not on the sabbath day." Well did Jesus speak to those who followed that command: "Strive to enter by the narrow gate."

"Go ahead," he said in irony, "give it a try. See if you can crawl into the kingdom of God by a narrow gate. You will never get there that way. Nobody ever does."

How Jesus understands the human side! How he knows that our off-the-mark nature tempts us to construct our narrow gates: "You can't be healed on the sabbath, so come another day;" "God will not accept you if you continue this behavior"; "Smile, or God won't love you."

Masters at creating narrow gates, we seek to control just how God can act among us. Narrow gates restrict, repress and block the flow of life.

Jesus himself is the householder who rises and shuts the narrow door of death. In his resurrection he closed the door of all human efforts to restrict and control the mercy of God. He cleared from the wide path of God's mercy all narrow and restrictive doors.

The narrow door, then, is not God's door at all. It is humankind's. It is primarily those relational gates we stick up in front of one another and in front of God, those roadblocks that keep life and love from flowing. Sometimes we will use our professional commitments to roadblock our interpersonal relationships. Sometimes we will use our interpersonal commitments to roadblock professional growth. The gates need not be so narrow. But they will be if we block out the grace, mercy and tenderness of God.

Why are our gates so narrow? What makes our gates so slim? Luther felt it was none other than the devil himself, the world and our own lazy flesh. We are resistant and defensive and we refuse to go on trusting God and clinging to his

Word. We make our lives to be like that of the medieval knight Tondalo, who in the legend had to cross a narrow bridge barely wider than a hand. Beneath him was a pit of sulphur full of dragons. Approaching him was someone to whom he had to yield. Luther goes on to say that the only way to cross our narrow bridges is to walk on, clinging to God's Word. His Word, a lamp unto our feet, will bring us home safely to the banquet of the kingdom of God. No narrow gate can restrict his Word. His Word is first; our gates are last. God's Word breaks our narrow gates wide open so his mercy, forgiveness and welcome can flow untrammeled to our hearts, just as he wishes it to be.

Ordinary Time 22
Luke 14:1, 7-14

Hold Your Peace?

Taylor Caldwell, in her book about Luke, *Dear and Glorious Physician,* tells how the gospel writer as a young boy sat near the window of his girlfriend, the daughter of a Roman tribune. Luke, in the story, a freed slave's son, really had no business in the courtyard of the tribune, no matter how he felt about his daughter.

As he stood there, leaning on a fountain in the courtyard, gazing toward the window of her room, he held in his hand a small, smooth stone. When the tribune noticed the boy he blurted out, "It is you, Lucanus!" The boy did not move. He did not move. He did not leap to his feet out of fear or respect. He simply sat there gazing, the stone in his hands. Finally he looked to the tribune and said, "I was praying for Rubria."

"You are praying for her? Well, she needs your prayers," said her father. "To what God did you pray?"

The boy replied softly, "To the unknown God."

When this fierce and ruddy Roman tribune surprised the small boy in his garden, the boy did not run away. Nor did he fold up like an armadillo and say nothing. He looked that giant of a man in the face and said clearly, "I am praying for your daughter." The young boy did not hold his peace.

In the gospels Jesus held his peace only once — when he stood face to face with that lascivious, wishy-washy King

Herod. Herod said, "Do me a miracle, Jesus of Nazareth. Here in my court, work me a miracle." And Jesus held his peace. It was not worth sharing with such a man.

The Pharisees and the scribes held their peace all the time. They never spoke out how they felt or what they thought. They held their peace — and pretended everything was just fine.

This passage from Luke takes place in a Pharisee's home — one of the chief Pharisees. Jesus went there on a sabbath to break bread with him. They were watching him. Pharisees were great watchers, especially of those whom they hated and feared.

And behold, there was a man before Jesus with dropsy, a disease that fills up the tissues and body cavities with fluids, a fatal disease.

Jesus looked around at all those people watching him and asked, "Is it lawful to heal on the sabbath day?" Luke tells us, "And they held their peace" (KJV). What gall these watchers had! Jesus asked a question and they would not say what they thought or what they felt. How difficult to deal with such people who don't say "Yes" or don't say "No." They just sit there holding their peace, like children sucking lollipops, exercising the backward power of inertia, irresistible forces and immovable objects all rolled into one.

We all have this power, and we use it to block the activity of God in our midst. God never holds his peace, especially in the face of inertia. That's when he heals and prompts and kicks his spurs in most of all.

A seminary professor once said the worst students were those who never asked any questions. He never knew where they stood on anything. After a while he began to realize they were afraid of what they thought and what they felt. They did not want their thoughts or feelings out in the marketplace with other people so they held their peace. Their fear eventually turned into hostility and hatred for their professor, especially when he asked them this question: "I know what other people think about this, but what do you think?"

Watched by those scribes and Pharisees who would not say what they thought or felt, Jesus made his move. He healed a man with dropsy and let him go. Then he asked those watchers a question: "If one of you has a child or an ox that has fallen into a well, will you not immediately pull it out on a sabbath day?" What did they say in response? They held their peace!

Their silence prompted Jesus' parable. When God invites men and women to the banquet of his kingdom he tells them, "Don't go directly to the center of the banquet where the guest of honor, Jesus, sits, risen and triumphant over death. If you go there right away you will do nothing but hold your peace. You will be so overawed that you will just sit there in fear, saying nothing to anyone, like the disciples when they met Jesus risen from the dead. No, first you need to taste the cross, the first course of my banquet. You need to start on the Good Fridays at the edge of the table, where light meets darkness, peace meets war, and little Jewish boys pray for little Greek girls. In anguish, turmoil and suffering, you will share your peace with one another. Through the cross, I will lead you to the center of my banquet, Jesus your Risen Lord."

The Pharisees watching Jesus that day traded the killing power of inertia corroding their relationships with God and with each other. Jesus traded the power of cross and resurrection inviting the poor, the maimed, the lame and the blind to God's banquet.

He invites us to the banquet as persons in need. Where we are poor he wants us to say so. Where we feel maimed he wants us to ask for help. Where we cannot walk in the paths God has set for us he wants us to pray, just as Luke prayed for his friend who was sick. We are all his beloved guests.

He wants us to come to his banquet, but not as one who holds his peace. Where we are poor he wants us to say so. Where we feel maimed inside he wants us to ask for help. Where we cannot walk in the paths he sets for us he wants us to speak out, just as little Luke did when he prayed for his friend who was ill.

Some preachers think this gospel passage was written by Emily Post or Miss Manners and not by Luke. The point of the parable is not proper etiquette, but faith.

In his undying faithfulness to us, God goes out to the highways and byways where we live. He goes inside of our hearts, beyond the fences we put up when we hold our peace. There, at the core of our hearts, God says, "Come to my banquet. Yes, I have a cross for you, but I have resurrection, too. I know your eyes grow dim, your hearts falter and your legs give way in fear, but I am with you. I am at your side and I will be with you until the end of time. Come and be nourished at my banquet."

Ordinary Time 23
Luke 14:25-33

Hate Your Mother And Father?

For many years American children sat down after supper each evening to snap on their radio dials. Sometimes they heard a sepulchre, Peter Lorre voice from a man named Raymond tell them about the "Inner Sanctum." On those nights America's children were scared. On other nights they waited with untrammeled glee until a man named McGee opened a closet door and years of clutter crashed to the living room floor. On those nights America's children were filled with great mirth. On yet another night, as they snapped on their Crosleys, Stromberg-Carlsons, or Zeniths, they waited with anxious breath until a woman's voice cried out, "Henry, Henry Aldrich," and a young teenager's voice answered, "Coming, Mother." On those nights America's children felt right at home.

Henry Aldrich did not hate his mother. So far as we know, he didn't hate his father either. In fact, he didn't hate anybody.

What, then, does Jesus mean in today's gospel when he says, "If anyone comes to me and does not hate his own father and mother and wife and children and brothers and sisters, yes, and even his own life, he cannot be my disciple"?

Coming back from Europe on a ship about 20 years ago, a young priest sat down one evening as a guest at the captain's table. The captain had been looking for someone to say mass on Sunday. Father Petrino volunteered, so he received this invitation in return. As he sat down, the first mate, an Italian, said, "Padre, before we sit down I want to tell you something. I hate all priests!" That was one of the rare times Father Petrino had heard anyone that clear and up front about the particular feeling called "Hate."

Is this what Jesus means? Are we to tell our mothers and fathers and sisters and brothers and wives, as we sit down to eat with them, "Before we begin this dinner tonight, mom and dad, sis and brother, I need to tell you something. I am now a disciple of Jesus and I hate all of you!"

That's not what Jesus has in mind. In this section of Luke's gospel, Jesus has just finished a dinner with one of the chief Pharisees. Let there be no mistake about it, the scribes and the Pharisees — at least some of them — did hate Jesus. No word better describes how they felt. They hated him because he called into question their priorities — their high value set on repression and control of the mercy, the kindness, and the tenderness of God. That's generally how hate grows anyway ... like a bacteria in a culture of repression and control.

No, Jesus has in mind something other than a dinner table scene where people tell each other how much they hold each other in contempt. After that dinner at the Pharisee's home, Jesus left, and great multitudes followed him. The gospel word for "multitudes" means a great crowd of harassed and troubled folk. What or who harassed and troubled these men and women? What Jesus said to them, as he turned, gives the clue: "If anyone comes after me and does not hate ..." "Hate" is not primarily a feeling word in the Aramaic language, the language Jesus spoke. It is primarily a priority word. It means to abandon or to leave aside; the way a sailor needs to abandon a sinking ship or the way a general needs to leave aside distracting things to win his battle.

This crowd following Jesus was harassed and troubled because they did not have their priorities straight. They needed to abandon the priorities of mother, father, brother, sister and wife to set up the priority of God. This crowd, still sailing on the sails of infancy and childhood, let the winds of family responsibility fill their sails instead of the Spirit of God. Familial expectations ran higher on the crest of their waves than hope from God. That's why they were harassed and troubled. Standing still, like Henry Aldrich at the foot of the hallway stairs, their lives were poised only to answer, "Coming, Mother!"

It is not easy for us to give up these natural priorities established when we were very young. Had not mother and father been priorities, then we would not have survived. There comes a day when priorities must alter, when the wind for our sails must come from another direction. The risky road of faith demands independence from family and the close companionship of God.

Martin Luther preached on this need we have to get out of our natural priorities and move on to God. "We work, we labor and we speculate," he said, "and we accomplish nothing else except to increase the restlessness of our souls. To all of us Christ says, 'You cannot refresh yourselves, but I can. Get out of yourselves and come to me. Despair of yourselves and hope in me, just as Abraham went out from his country, his kindred, and his father's house.' "[1]

No such confusion in Jesus. The priorities were straight. A little later on in this gospel account Jesus met the rich young ruler who did not kill, steal, or commit adultery. He honored his father and his mother. "One thing you still lack," said Jesus, "sell all that you have. Negotiate in the marketplace your non-murderous, non-thieving, non-adulterous life. Barter with other men and women the honor you hold for your mother and father. Give that honor to the others who need honor from you (the gospel calls these people 'poor') and you will begin to have treasure in heaven. Then, come, follow me."

The rich young man couldn't do it. He had all those things in such abundance he felt he could never give them up. So much was invested in his life of no murders, no thefts and no adultery he could not trade it away for a more positive life. Honor for mother and father held him like a bear trap. He could not abandon that ship to sail on freer seas. His face fell; he was very sad.

Clutching the gold of his personal priorities, he valued his commandments more than his independence. Honor of mother and father weighed more heavily on the scale than his own freedom. Jesus said to Peter and his disciples, after meeting this rich young ruler, "Truly, I say to you, there is no one who has left house or wife or brothers or parents or children for the sake of the kingdom of God who will not receive manifold more in this time and in the age to come, eternal life."

The freedom of the individual believer — that's what Jesus meant when he said to the troubled crowd, "Hate your mother and father." He didn't say, "Kill them," "rob them," "make war on them," or "blast them off the map." He said simply, "Leave them aside. Abandon them when they become a sinking ship for you. Let them go when they are a distraction in your battles. Only God will ever be your steady ship. Only God will lead you, like a general, free."

It is so easy to be beguiled in all this. Family is so natural and the bonds are so strong. Family life, claiming energy, time, property and resources, sets the familiar and comfortable course. God's call reaches beyond the path of family ties. His demands are greater, but so are his rewards — purpose, direction and the glorious liberty of the children of God.

Why, then, stand at the foot of the hallway stairs all our lives long? Jesus' good news says, "Move on. Abandon that ship. Its hull has rotted and its sails are torn. Stay on the ship of family and you will never leave port. Stay on the ship of God and you will sail forever."

---

1. *Luther's Works*, 51 (Muhlenberg, 1959), pp. 29-30.

Ordinary Time 24
Luke 15:1-10

The Other Ninety-nine

A few years ago on a small farm in Ohio, a young woman waited anxiously for her husband to come home. Usually he returned about 5:30 for supper, but not this day. Linda called his place of business. He had left at the regular hour. Six thirty came. Still no husband. At 7:30 she put her two small children to bed. As she peered through the window toward the setting sun, the fields were rich with budding grain, but no one came up the road toward the home. Eight thirty rolled by, nine thirty. She called the sheriff's office. At 11:30 the sheriff knocked on her door. Her husband had been found in a nearby barn, where he had taken his own life.

Shocked beyond belief, Linda reeled through the next few weeks, intoxicated with grief. Then her emotions froze. As they did she began to notice the little boy whom she had put to bed at 7:30 that night. Scott withdrew and became moody. He missed his father very much. In his tears he ran to his grandfather. Everyone, especially a five-year-old fatherless boy, needs a shepherd.

Linda decided to move back with her parents in Idaho. The day they left Ohio, Scott cried and cried. He did not want to leave his shepherd.

Two weeks after they arrived in northern Idaho, Scott disappeared. His mother, frantic, called the neighbors. They called the police. Her little boy was lost, she said, and she didn't know where to find him. Finally a police helicopter spotted him walking along an abandoned railroad track.

"I'm not lost," he said, "I know where I am going. I'm going back to see my grandfather." He was going back to his shepherd.

In today's gospel parable, Jesus defies a group of murmuring scribes and Pharisees, cooing like pigeons on a church steeple about Jesus' search for lost sheep.

Walking down the railroad tracks in Jesus' day were men collecting Roman taxes and women wearing alabaster jars around their necks — lost sheep in a pharisaical world.

The Pharisees, of course, never walked those tracks. "We are safe in the sheepfold," they said. "We know where the pasture is and we are never lost." Who needs a shepherd when we, the sheep, are in control?"

How abhorrent to a Pharisee, a lost sheep. Nothing turned their stomachs more than those tax collecting men and those alabastered women, the lost sheep of Israel.

The gospel word we translate as "lost" really means destroyed, utterly devastated, crushed by a rock or chased from the flock. The tax collectors and prostitutes Jesus sought after did not just wander away. They were chased away. They did not just fall off the edge of a cliff. They were pushed off. They did not leave the flock. They were driven out.

Jesus, going after them, did not leave the 99 in the sheepfold where the wolf could not enter in. Nor did he secure them in a rich pasture. He abandoned them in a desert where wolves ran wild and no grass grew. Jesus knew from experience that no one finds nourishment or protection in the desert unless it comes from God. The 99 had something to learn.

The 99 were too self-sufficient and too much in control. They needed God only to control him. Secure in the sheepfold of their own good works, they measured grace, ounce by ounce, as their reward for what they had accomplished. Their own study of the law refreshed them by day and gave them fire by night. To God they murmured, "No thank you, Lord, we'll make our own light in the darkness and our own rainfall when we feel dry. And we will drive from the sheepfold any lambs who feel differently about you."

So God abandoned them. He left them to themselves and went after the lamb who longed for God to be his light by night, his rainfall by day. Running after his rejected sheep, God left behind the 99 in the desert. Why? So they, too, could feel how much they really needed God in their lives. No one controls God. No one is that self-sufficient.

Scott, walking on that railroad track in northern Idaho, did not walk that track on his own. He was pushed out there by the woman who did not want him around. Scott's mother was finding him a bother and a distraction. When he cried about his father she sent him to his room without supper. One day, instead of going to school, he started for Ohio, where he knew his shepherd was. His mother had become a Pharisee. Steeled in her own grief, she could not stomach her little boy's tears.

God left this Pharisee mother in the desert as he prompted the boy to take to the tracks for Ohio. "Now," God thought, "she will see how precious this boy is to me. She will feel something of the compassion I feel for him. In stifling his tears she is driving this precious lamb of mine from me — his pillar of fire by night and his cloud of refreshment by day. I will leave her in the desert for a while. She will learn she is not sufficient unto herself or in control of my lambs. She will learn to cry."

God does this to us all. When we are self-sufficiently safe in the sheepfold or fat in the pasture, he will take someone away. Feeling left behind in the desert we will go to God for light and seek the protection of his nourishing Word. Only when we are left in the desert will we run to the shepherd for the help we need.

Martin Luther often felt driven to the desert. He called such times his "anfechtung," his inner sense of turmoil, pain, and loss. Luther felt these feelings came from God who sometimes plays with us in a friendly manner to tease us. At such times Luther liked to read, pray and sing psalms.

When Scott came back to Linda, they prayed together. She took her son in her arms and held him so tightly he felt she would never let him go. God melted away the wall of her sheepfold that day and sprouted grass in the desert of her heart, bathed now by the waters of their mingled tears.

Ordinary Time 25
Luke 16:1-13

Ashamed
To Beg

In a large attractive office in a major city, a man worked for several months next to a small attractive woman. He had been there only a few days when he thought he'd ask her to lunch, which he did. The following day he asked her for dinner and they began a long dating relationship. They went to craft fairs together, since he liked to do that. They went to the ocean, which he also liked to do. They used to take long walks along the river.

He liked this relationship. He had lived for many years with his mother. In fact, it was only a few months after she died that he began dating his co-worker. Little by little, however, she began to dislike both the relationship and this man. She felt like she really wasn't herself when she was with him. She couldn't speak what she really felt. She rarely asserted where she wanted to go or what she wanted to do. She later said, "I just wasn't Sandra with him."

So she terminated her social, dating relationship with this man. Once she did, she began to feel like herself again. Her friends told her, "You're more like the old Sandra now."

Across the same town, in another office, a young man sat at his desk for eight years, struggling to manage his office work force. Outside he was a friendly, generous person. In the office he was the same way and his workers flattened him out, like steamrollers over an asphalt road. He worked long, long hours; he holed himself up behind his desk to keep all the records accurate; he just about wore himself out. Finally his friends told him, "Steve, you'd better get out of that job. You're not yourself anymore. Those people are eating you alive and you're not getting anywhere."

He protested, "But it's a good job. I make good money. And besides, it is what I do best. How can I even look for anything else?"

Then the company was sold. New management came in. All the supervisors were replaced and Steve found himself on the street. He was terrified. "To dig I am unable, to beg I am ashamed," he said. "What can I do?"

His friends told him they were glad he was fired. "At least you are your old self," they said. "And you'll find something. Just go for it." He did, and now he's doing better than he ever could have in the position he once felt he could never leave.

The steward in this passage from Luke's gospel is like both Sandra and Steve. Sandra was not herself in that relationship. Steve was not himself in that job. Both were wasting away, losing that which was most precious to them both: their proper identities. Both felt they could not survive if they gave up something so close and precious as a relationship or a job.

In this particular passage the steward's master calls him on the carpet. In Luke's mind, this Lord and Master is God. God always calls his stewards into question when they are wasteful of who and what they are. This steward is not just wasting his master's goods. The steward is wasting himself. Nothing is more precious in God's household than his steward's proper identity. This is God's gift to this steward, and he is wasting it. No wonder God calls him to account.

God does this to us all the time. He checks our relationships and he checks our jobs — to help us make sure we are not wasting our identities where we are. This steward was. So God dismissed him. He had to get a new job and a new relationship. God does not tolerate our wasting who we are.

This dismissal turned the light on for the steward. "What shall I do? To dig I am unable, to beg I am ashamed." Finally he came to an assessment of who he was and what he could do. He came to value his own identity, one of his master's most precious goods.

He called in his master's creditors. "How much do you owe? One hundred barrels of oil? Take your bill and write 50." Did he cheat his master? Not at all. The commercial documents from that time indicate that 50 percent was the normal commission. He renounced what he thought he had to have to live on — and he won friends for himself in so doing.

"How much do you owe? One hundred bushels of wheat? Take your bill and write 80." He did not cheat his master. He simply renounced his own commission. He gave up what he thought he needed to survive, and he survived much better without it. He zeroed in on his own identity, rather than on the commission he thought he had to have to survive.

Bruno Bettelheim, who has studied the survivors of the concentration camps in World War II, writes that those who survived were able to give up everything they thought they needed and, in so giving, they survived. Those who thought they would die if they had no clothing, no jewelry, no regular food, no books — they did not make it.

Sometimes God will do to us what he did to this steward. He will strip us down to the very core of our existence to make us discover who we really are. He will bring us to a crossroad in life where we will be forced to say, "To dig I am not able, to beg I am ashamed." There God will reveal to us who we are. As we reach to him for help we will find ourselves renouncing our commissions — whatever we think we need to survive but we really don't. God knows that.

This passage from Luke introduces that curious term, "mammon," an Aramaic word which means: "that in which I put my trust." We are like Sandra, Steve, and this steward. How easy to put all our trust in relationships or commissions or a job. God will not let us do that forever. He will force us to give up those people and those things we feel are absolutely critical. In God's eyes they are roadblocks to the truth. He will take them away. Then we will discover our real identities as God's stewards, and him alone shall we serve.

Ordinary Time 26
Luke 16:19-31

Desires
Bring Hope

An old man died in a Manhattan brownstone some years ago. No one in the neighborhood knew much about him. Some neighbors thought he was odd and eccentric. Most ignored him altogther. Just a silly recluse, they said. When he died the newspapers sent a reporter to his brownstone home. Inside they found newspapers and magazines stacked to the ceilings. Narrow corridors wound in a maze throughout the house. When the papers and magazines were removed, furniture of all kinds, including 17 grand pianos were found buried in that labyrinth of debris. Langley Collier had acquired a great fortune but he lived as a recluse in his home, buried in canyons of newspapers and debris.

The rich man in this passage from Luke was not like Langley Collier. He did not live in a canyon of debris. Nor did he spend his life like a recluse. The poor man was like Langley Collier, for the word we translate as "poor man" means one who hides himself from other people.

Langley Collier chose to live hidden in that brownstone with his 17 grand pianos and all those magazines. Like him the poor man in the gospel hid himself. He was afraid. He was so afraid of other people that he would not ask for anything. He would not even go to the rich man's table where he could get something to eat. His friends had to bring him there. He was afraid to go by himself.

The poor man did have one thing going for him, however. The poor man had desires. Great desires. The same longings and desires the prodigal son felt. When he watched the swine he was feeding stuff themselves with corn husks, he desired to feed on them as well. This the poor man desired — to feed on the bread that fell from the rich man's table.

Then something happened to both the poor man and the rich man in this story. They both died. Death brought the poor man with desires to the bosom of Abraham. It brought the rich man, with no desires, to hades — or to hell.

The New Testament word for hell means "not to see anything," especially not to see anything that our fears and our feelings lead us to see. That's what death did to the rich man. It opened his eyes to see that he had been living in a world where he respected neither his feelings nor his fears. He lived only as the elder brother of the prodigal son — enslaved to duty and resentful of his brother's deep desires. "Father Abraham," he cried out, "have mercy upon me, and send Lazarus to dip the tip of his finger in water and cool my tongue, for I am anguished in this flame."

Did he die physically? Is that what brought this change to his life? Or did he die emotionally? Did something happen in his life where suddenly he was no longer comfortable feasting sumptuously day by day? Was hell really a new place for him — or just a new perspective on the old familiar places?

The point of this story is not "after-life." The point of the gospel is "now-life." Now — where the kingdom of God is, in and among us. God brought some kind of death to the rich man and to the poor man alike. They both needed some kind of radical separation in their lives: the poor man to stop being such a recluse and to enjoy the intimacy of life in the bosom of Abraham; the rich man to stop living a life that had only a full belly but no desires!

The rich man says, "I am in this place of torment." He does not want his brothers to come to this place. The word indicates that the rich man now experiences life as a head wind into which he must sail or as a sea that tosses him about.

That's why God brought this death experience, this sense of loss into his life — precisely so he would start living like a ship sailing into the wind, tossed to and fro on the sea. Life in the banquet hall is no life at all from God's perspective; life on the high seas is.

Some years ago a man's youngest son died at the age of 18. The boy had been retarded and his father had devoted his entire life to the care of his son. After he died, the father grew morose and dejected. "I have nothing to live for," he said. He died himself, very young, a few years later. A man without desires is already dead. That's why God will bring him to the place of torment, where the winds blow and the seas toss — to bring desires back into his life.

Neither the rich man nor the poor man is the hero in this story. God is. The poor man is a frightened rabbit. The rich man is a strutting peacock. They both need God. They both need Moses and the prophets. They both need to listen.

Significant changes in our lives come only when we experience a great sense of loss and then start to listen to Moses and the prophets again. Then God fans the flames of desire in our hearts again.

Many years ago a missionary returned from India. He noted a big difference between the Jewish-Christian religious tradition and that of the Hindus. The Hindu scriptures encourage the stifling of all desire. The god Krishna says, "Kill the enemy menacing you in the form of desire. Desire obscures knowledge like dirt in a mirror."

In our Judaeo-Christian tradition desire holds a high place. The poor man desires intimacy and the nourishment that it brings, but he cannot create intimacy himself. God has to drag him through the needle of a death first. Then he can rest in the bosom of Abraham. The rich man has no desires. God drags him, too, through the same needle and then his wishes begin.

God wants us neither to be rich men with no desires nor poor men afraid to seek what we desire. He wants us to have ears straining to hear his word and hearts longing for his love.

Much of the steam for the reformation in the days of Martin Luther came from his burning desire to open the ears and hearts of Europe once again to God's Word and love. In Luther's day, too, many Christians were either surfeited with their own good works and therefore did not listen, or they were living like frightened rabbits and therefore did not love. God, by raising up Luther, drew the whole of European Christianity through the needle of death to the old ways so that the priority of God's Word and love could be established again.

God's Word penetrates our hearts like a two-edged sword to keep us from living as isolates, hidden under the rubble of our fears, and to stir up in us a deep and endless desire for his abiding love.

Ordinary Time 27
Luke 17:5-10

Millstones And Mustard Seeds

One bright day in March a young man awoke at 4:30 a.m. Crystal clear sunlight poured into Jack's room, like a great river leading him to a new day. He was too high up for any river to flow — springs or small streams, yes, but no rivers. Kurseong, not far from Darjeeling, stood 8,000 feet above sea level, in the foothills of the Himalayas. As he rubbed his eyes in that radiant dawn, he looked out his window to the highest spot on the face of the earth. There, far in the distance, sparkling like a diamond in the sky, shone Mount Everest, The highest mountain in all the world. What a glorious feeling to see that peak in that clear morning light.

Jack was in India for his cousin Marty's ordination. Years before, when Marty had volunteered for the missions, he had been sent to Nepal, where he served as headmaster of the high school. Now he was in Kurseong for his ordination and Jack was with him. Marty liked carpentry much more than anything else. In his days as a seminary student he had set up a carpentry shop in the village where he taught those skills to the village children.

The same morning, as the two cousins walked to the village through the woods, they noticed strange objects hanging from the trees — small blue rectangular frames, criss-crossed with blue, red, green and orange threads. The criss-crossing was so meticulous and so closely wound that even a fly could not pass through. Jack asked his cousin, "What are those things?" "Spirit traps," he said.

"Spirit traps?"

"Yes, the people in Kurseong believe in spirits. Their village has its spirit, as does our seminary. They don't want the seminary spirits getting into their village, so they set traps all through the woods to make sure our spirits keep to themselves!"

"Spirit traps." When Jesus said to his disciples, "Temptations must come," he was talking about traps. The word we translate as "temptation" comes from the Greek word that means "trap" or "stumbling block." Why did Jesus speak of temptations as "traps" at this point in the gospel? He knew his disciples were like little rabbits, about to run into snares, and he had to warn them to be on their guard.

Who was setting the traps? First of all, the high priests and the Sadducees set one for Judas. The bait was 30 pieces of silver, and they knew he would go for it. Once they gave that silver to Judas they began to feel the millstone around their necks. Their power and influence was over. A few years later the Roman legions wiped them out. Traps we set for other people always have a way of coming back home, like chickens to their roost. Once Judas snared Jesus in the kiss of betrayal, the millstone wrapped itself around his neck, too. He went out and hanged himself. "Temptation — 'traps' — must come," said Jesus, "But woe to him by whom they come!"

Who else was setting traps?

The woman in the high priest's courtyard, warming herself by the fire, set one for Peter. "You were with him," she said. "Why, your speech betrays you. You, too, are a Galilean!" Peter snared in the trap of denial cried out, "I know not the man!" Jesus looked at him and Peter wept bitterly. Legend has it that the furrows from those tears remained on his face the rest of his life. Peter felt a millstone around his neck as he realized he had denied his friend, but those hot tears streaming down his face dissolved it and washed it away. Tears have a way of doing that.

Hearing this, the disciples were afraid. "Increase our faith!" they said. "We can't believe this. We cannot believe that such things will happen." They knew that faith had power. They had seen the woman with the 12-year flow of blood touch the hem of his garment, and immediately be healed. "Your faith has made you well," he said. "Go in peace." To the sinful woman who had bathed his feet with her tears he had said, "Your sins are forgiven. Your faith has saved you. Go in peace."

With the traps of betrayal and denial set clearly on the road ahead, no wonder the disciples wanted more faith. They wanted to be healed of their propensities to fall into traps. They wanted to go in peace.

Sometimes the snares in our lives are like those around that seminary in Kurseong — little wire webs to keep us from moving into villages where it would be helpful for us to go.

Only faith — the disciples were right — can save us from such snares. Traps will be set. We will be encouraged to betray our loyalties and deny those whom we love. Someone is setting the traps now. It is part of human nature to set the traps, and it is part of human nature to step into them.

Enter the mustard seed. In India people have been known to chew on narcotic seeds all day long. It is a great concern to the missionaries, for these seeds dull all feeling. The mustard seed is not like that. If you chew on a mustard seed, you don't have a decrease of feeling, you have an increase. If you put enough mustard seed into a soup, you won't taste anything else!

"Have faith like a mustard seed," said Jesus. "Leave behind your fondness for the dull tastes of betrayal and denial. Rather, let the hot, stinging taste of faith be on your tongue, and let that be what directs you in your life — fidelity not betrayal, loyalty not denial — and you will begin to see the symcimine trees in your life jump from the land and plant themselves in the sea ... such is the marvel of God's gift of faith.

The traps are out there. We can't live as human beings without them. They will be set and we will fall into them —

betrayal traps and denial traps. We all feel these things in our lives. Faith puts the taste of God on our tongues so that, with the Lord as our ship's captain, we can be spirited to sail through these traps to the brighter land.

Extraordinary Faith
For Ordinary Time

Larry R. Kalajainen

Introduction

On December 31, thousands of people will gather in Times Square in New York City to watch the big red apple, symbol of that exciting and turbulent metropolis, descend slowly down the pole atop of which it sits precisely at the stroke of midnight. Millions more will watch the annual ritual on television. Horns will blow, the crowds will cheer, many will embrace and kiss their partners, throw confetti, or toast one another with champagne. A new year will elbow its way onstage, though apart from the change of the calendar, the minute after midnight will differ in no observable way from the minute before midnight. Yet everything will have changed. The old year will be gone forever. It will hold no more possibilities. It is used-up time — past time. The future looms ahead, dark, mysterious, yet full of promise.

However, for Christians, the new year will have already begun some five weeks earlier on the first Sunday in Advent. The observances marking the passing of the old year and the onset of the new will have been markedly different. In contrast to the noisy and boisterous New Year's parties that mark the turning of the calendar, Christians will celebrate their New Year by lighting Advent candles, singing hymns, and offering prayers.

These differences of observance are more significant than they might at first appear. For Christians, the liturgical calendar is not simply a different way of measuring time; it signifies a different way of living in time. Christians measure time, not by months or days or years, but by seasons of the gospel. The yearly commemoration of the birth, life, ministry, death, and resurrection of Jesus are the mileposts that define the quality of time for us. The great gospel events fill time with meaning; they mark time as not merely *chronos* — the passage of time — but as *kairos* — the fullness of time or the opportune time.

The gospel seasons are named for their relationship to the great feasts of Christ's nativity, his passion, and his resurrection. Advent, Christmas, Epiphany, Lent, Holy Week, Easter, and Pentecost are the drumbeats that march us through the days, teaching us to keep time to gospel rhythms.

But the celebration of these gospel feasts does not occupy the whole year. Between Epiphany and Lent are some weeks that have no name. Trinity Sunday leads ... where? A long succession of unnamed weeks stretches ahead until Christ the King Sunday finally brings the liturgical year to its close. These Sundays, which are not related to any of the gospel feasts, are designated "Ordinary Time."

Ordinary time sounds as though it might mean insignificant time. Time when nothing important is happening. Time like any other time. Time that does not demand any particular way of living. Time that is not invested with eternity.

But nothing could be further from the truth. All of time is now sacred time because of the mighty acts of God in Jesus Christ which the major feasts celebrate. We are ordinary people, and ordinary time is a gift to us. It offers us opportunity to practice living by the grace notes of the gospel seasons. It is time filled, not with meanings assigned to it by the gospel events, but with the meanings that we give to it as we live in time as Christ's disciples. God has invested time with meaning, and we celebrate that meaning in the gospel seasons. But we also have an investment to make in time. Ordinary time is our time. It is ours to fill with meaning, with purpose, with faithful discipleship, with love. It is our time to respond to God's revelation and redemption in Christ. It is we who make ordinary time holy. If these meditations for the last third of the church year can help you discover the faith to live an extraordinary life in ordinary time, they will have fulfilled their purpose.

Larry R. Kalajainen
Paris, France

Ordinary Time 28
Luke 17:11-19

The Saving Power Of Gratitude

On the old television show "All In The Family," there was an episode when Archie Bunker's son-in-law Mike, or "Meathead" as Archie always called him, asks Archie a riddle. "A young man is seriously injured in an accident and is rushed to the hospital for emergency surgery. When the surgeon is called, it turned out that the young man was the son of the surgeon, but the surgeon was not the boy's father." Archie suggests that the boy was adopted, or that the surgeon was his step-father. But with a triumphant glint in his eye, Mike informs Archie that the surgeon was the boy's mother. Good old Archie, the archetypal male chauvinist, would never have seen the answer to that one. His presuppositions blinded him to the obvious.

The prophet Micah, many centuries ago, proclaimed some obvious, but unpleasant realities to people who were likewise blinded to the truth of their situation by their suppositions. They were solid, middle-class citizens of Jerusalem, morally upright, religious, and socially respectable. They thought God was in their camp, and that their prosperity was the sign of God's favor. But Micah told them otherwise. Their prosperity, he told them, was the result of their having coveted their poorer and weaker neighbors' fields and houses. They seized what they wanted, enriching themselves at the expense of those weaker. But God, who sees what proud and greedy human beings do not, stands over against such pride and power, and takes the part of the weak and the poor. God's judgment is not based on human standards, but on God's own truth and righteousness, and God makes it clear that oppression and exploitation will bear its own bitter fruit.

The people, of course, do not want to hear this message of the prophet. "Don't preach this way," they tell him, "One should not preach this way; disgrace will not overtake us" (Micah 2:6). Micah, however, rages against such moral and spiritual blindness and presumption. Sarcastically he tells them that the sort of preacher they want is someone who will tell them about the evils of drinking liquor. That's always a good, safe topic for a preacher. After all, who can argue with homilies about the benefits of sobriety? His listeners are probably the most sober people around. Of course they'll listen to homilies on the evils of drunkenness. Such homilies are aimed at somebody else, and those are the homilies that all of us want to hear.

It's easy to be morally outraged at the drug traffic in our inner cities, at the corruption and degradation of the welfare system, at the city schools that are more often battlegrounds than they are places of education, at the racial violence that erupts spectacularly in places like Los Angeles. It's easy to point fingers and assign blame to a particular ethnic group or political party, a particular civic leader or government program. What we don't want to hear is that we ourselves are responsible. That is not something we want to deal with. We don't personally wish to be oppressive or exploitative, we don't personally engage in greedy or overly self-indulgent lifestyles, and so we don't want to hear that we are all, in some way, responsible, or that we are likely to experience the judgment that is inherent in the injustices of our society. Even if we are willing to hear about our own complicity in the oppressive structures of our social order, we often feel helpless to do anything about it. What can one person, or even one congregation, do about such massive, structural and systematic problems?

Our gospel passage, which is the story of Jesus and the healing of ten people with leprosy, may give us some clues. At first, when I read the scripture readings for this weekend, I was stumped. What on earth did this story in Luke's gospel have to do with Micah's harsh indictment of the good, solid, middle-class citizens of ancient Jerusalem? But the more I reflected on them, the more I began to see some connections — not only connections between the two passages of scripture, but connections to my own life and to our life together as the Body of Christ.

The first clue that may hint at some connections is the simple fact that Jesus, in stark contrast to all the social taboos of his day, stopped to listen to the request of a group of lepers. Today, we know that leprosy is not only easily curable with the right medication, but is not very contagious at all. In fact, if one person were married to another who had an active case of Hansen's disease, which is the medical name for leprosy, there would only be a five percent chance of contagious infection. But because leprosy is such a disfiguring disease, it was greatly feared, and in the ancient world, and even today, it is accompanied by strong social taboos. In Jesus' day, to even come into close proximity to a leper was to risk spiritual pollution. And to touch a leper was to incur such pollution that exaggerated rituals of cleansing would be necessary before one was allowed back into polite company. Even the strong enmity between Jews and Samaritans was overcome by the stronger social taboo of leprosy. Nine of the ten lepers were Jews; one was a Samaritan. Their common affliction brought them into community with each other — a community of the socially damned.

It's not difficult to see parallels between the social taboos against leprosy in Jesus' day, and the social taboos against victims of AIDS in our own, is it? *Moody Monthly,* a Christian magazine, reported the story of a woman who called a church and asked the pastor if he would please pray for her son. "Of course, I will," replied the pastor. "Is there something in particular I should pray for?" The mother replied, "He has AIDS. And this is the fifth church I've called to find someone willing to pray for my son. The first two ministers I talked to hung up on me when I told them my son's problem. One simply said no, and one didn't call back when I left a message on the answering machine.''

Jesus stopped to listen to a group of people who were the silenced people of his day. The social outcasts. The pariahs. Others went out of their way to avoid any contact with lepers. Jesus stopped, listened, and responded to their request for healing. He went against the grain of his own society's rules and taboos. He risked social ostracism himself in order to minister to those silenced ones, those who were excluded from polite company.

A second clue is in the response of those healed. Ten lepers were healed; nine of them followed Jesus' instructions to go show themselves to the priests in the temple at Jerusalem. To the priests was committed the responsibility for admitting or excluding someone from the community. Since leprosy excluded a person from the community, a priest had to pronounce that a person was cured of leprosy in order for him to be readmitted into society. So the nine lepers did what Jesus told them, went to the priests, and presumably were readmitted into society and became solid middle-class citizens once again. And although Luke doesn't say so directly, it might not be stretching the point too far to think that once readmitted, they might have conformed to society's values and taboos themselves. They probably took up despising Samaritans again just like the rest of polite society.

But one leper came back to Jesus to thank him and to give praise to God for his healing. And to top it off, he was the doubly damned one — the Samaritan. Jesus expressed astonishment that the only one who had enough gratitude to praise God for his healing was this despised foreigner, this one who was double the outsider, both because of his leprosy and because he was a Samaritan. And Jesus' statement to this grateful man hits us like a stroke of lightning. "Go your way, your faith has saved you." Jesus had already healed him of leprosy. But now, he receives something more as a result of his gratitude to God for the blessing of the recovery of his health and readmission to human society: salvation — the wholeness of life, the total well-being that comes to those who depend entirely upon God and not on themselves. That's the word that is used in Jesus' statement — the word salvation. Jesus equates this man's gratitude with faith, faith in God, dependence upon God, trust in God's mercy, and that is the attitude which brings him the blessing of salvation.

The final clue to the connections between this story and Micah's prophecy, and the clue to the connections to our own lives comes in Jesus' answer to the question raised by the Pharisees immediately following this story. It's no accident that Luke places this question and answer right after the story of the salvation of the grateful leper. The Pharisees are the morally upright, deeply religious, and socially respectable citizens of their day. Solid people. Good people. They ask Jesus, "When is the kingdom of God coming?" Jesus replies, "The kingdom of God is not coming with spectacular signs; in fact, the kingdom of God is among you." What does this mean? It means that the kingdom of God is present where we are least disposed to look, especially if we're the solid, respectable, morally upright, hard-working, salt-of-the-earth types that we are. It means that we probably ought not to be blinded like the people of Micah's day and think that our prosperity and our solid middle-class values and the fact that we're sober and not drunken sots are the signs of God's kingdom. Rather, the signs of God's kingdom are when people like us, out of gratitude, begin to pay attention to the outcasts, to the silenced, to the socially unacceptable. When we overcome our fears and taboos to minister to AIDS victims, when we offer our time and energies to providing for the needs of children damaged because their parents were drug addicts, when we open our doors to the poor and welcome them among us, when we work for better housing and better health care, even though it may mean paying higher taxes to make it possible, and when we do it because we are grateful that we ourselves have been healed and touched by God, then we know that the kingdom of God is among us.

I know of an urban congregation, an old "downtown" church, which took some bold steps in 1987 to reach out to the silenced and excluded people of the inner city. Most of them were not residents of the inner city themselves. For the most part, they were respectable, middle-class people who lived in the suburbs. But their church had been standing on the central square of the city for many years. Through all the prosperity of the '50s, the social revolution of the '60s and the urban blight of the '70s, they had stayed downtown because they knew they had a mission there, even if it wasn't always clear to them what it was or how to go about it.

But it was becoming obvious that they needed help to fulfill it. And so, in cooperation with a sister church in the affluent suburbs, they began an Urban Mission Project amid many uncertainties, with inadequate planning, inadequate funds, and little idea where it would all lead, if anywhere. And God honored that vision. They hired a full-time staff person skilled in urban ministry to coordinate their efforts. The program, however, was dependent upon the participation of many volunteers from the two congregations.

With financial strain an ever-present companion, they began ministries with inner city children, homeless men, and welfare mothers — ministries which have brought hope and transformed lives to many who were without hope. Before that bold step, people in the city used to ask if there was still an active congregation at that church; it always looked as though it were closed. Now, no one asks that question. Now that church is known as the church which is "doing something" in the city, and other churches and city officials alike look to that congregation for a model of what ordinary people who care can do.

When asked why they took such a risk of faith to reach out to people at the bottom of the social and economic ladder, many of those who volunteer in the various ministries simply reply that they feel it's the least they can do in light of all of God's blessings which they enjoy. In other words, they are grateful. Gratitude motivates them and enables them to be beacons of hope to those without hope.

D. T. Niles, the Indian theologian, once defined evangelization as "one hungry beggar telling another hungry beggar where to find bread." When we are grateful enough for the bread that we have received that we are willing to reach out to the lost and hurting and lonely and excluded ones around us, we will discover that we ourselves are being saved.

Ordinary Time 29
Luke 18:1-8

Tough Faith In Tough Times

Two qualities which we Americans value highly and in which we take pride are speed and efficiency. Think of how many products or services which all of us use that are built principally around one or both of these qualities. Hundreds of thousands of microwave ovens have been sold, not because they make food taste better, but because it's possible to cook much faster in them. Since so many people lead such busy lives, anything that shortens time in the kitchen has an instant appeal.

A colleague told of meeting a woman from West Germany at a seminar on prayer in Princeton. She was marvelling over one of our speedy and efficient inventions, the tea bag. She said that the Germans don't make teabags, and she found it a very convenient way to have a cup of tea. Of course, she then went on to mention that teabags didn't produce nearly as tasty a cup of tea as loose tea does.

Our banking procedures are also marvels of efficiency. A friend who served as a missionary in Malaysia always used to complain that it took him anywhere from 20-45 minutes to cash his paycheck because of the inefficient banking procedures. Instead of having each teller be a cashier as we do, the tellers and the cashiers were different people. The teller looked over your check, made sure that your deposit slip was filled out correctly, got the initials of one of the bank officers on the cashier's approval slip, and then placed it on the bottom of the pile of similar checks waiting to be cashed by the cashier who sat enclosed in a little cubicle. After standing in line at the teller's counter, one then went over and stood in line at the cashier's counter, and waited some more. Cashing a paycheck was a great lesson in patience each month, a quality that we Americans are notably short on.

Because of our cultural preference for speed and efficiency, our gospel lesson this morning has something to say to us that each of us needs very much to hear. The themes of patient waiting, of persistence, of faithfulness in the face of the seeming indifference of God to our troubles are addressed by this rather strange story in Luke's gospel.

The story of the "unjust judge" as it's often called, raises an age-old human question: why, if God is righteous, is he so slow in seeing that justice is done? Why does it seem like justice is constantly perverted? Why doesn't God act quickly and efficiently to rectify injustice and vindicate those who are righteous and punish those who are wicked? It's probably the most common human complaint and question there is, isn't it? Is there any one of us who hasn't asked it scores of times?

When we read in *Newsweek* about the terrible situation in Bosnia, we ask, "Why doesn't God intervene in some way?" When we hear of the massacres of innocent people including children in Rwanda and Burundi, we shiver at the horror of it all and wonder why the people of those lands cannot see that ancient rivalries are preventing them from achieving prosperity in the modern world.

Closer to home, we see the blight in our inner cities; we deplore the violence that is so frequently related to the drug traffic in areas of poverty. Since our orientation is toward problem-solving, we look for immediate solutions. Get tough on drug dealers. Mandatory prison sentences, more police, cut off aid to Colombia. Yet our solutions don't seem to solve the problem. They have the virtue of speed and efficiency, but the problems themselves prove more recalcitrant and intractable than we imagined. Because we lack patience and the persistence to search for solutions that may not be speedy and efficient, but which, in the long term, would be more effective, we become frustrated and lose interest. Long-term issues don't have much media appeal.

The same holds true for our personal lives as for our social and international problems. Our washing machine breaks down, and we immediately call the repairman. Problem solved. But let us break a hip or develop a heart condition, and we lose patience quickly. We get depressed or we become complainers. We want to be back at full steam, and we don't like having to wait.

Jesus' parable of the persistent widow and the unjust judge offers a corrective to our impatience and our fascination with short-term problem-solving. The experience of the widow is one which is instantly familiar to us. We've all known the frustrations of delay in having our needs and wants gratified. We've all known what it's like to be treated unjustly; we've all known what it's like to have our plea for fairness, for justice, go unheard or unheeded. Those who have ever tried to reason with an IRS auditor know exactly how this poor widow felt. The cards were stacked against her. The judge may even have been in league with her opponent who was exploiting her in some way. The widow cries to the judge for justice, and the only reason she eventually gets it is because the judge gets weary of listening to her lament. She wears him down with her persistence until he finally does the right thing just to get rid of her.

Interpreters of this parable have sometimes made the mistake of turning this parable into an allegory, assigning the role of the judge to God. Not only does that cause us to miss the main point, it also casts God in a very unflattering light. The parable does urge us to be like the widow, praying persistently without giving up. But the only point of contact between God and the judge is one of contrast. God is *not* like the unjust judge, and God's response to our persistent requests will not be like the response of the unjust judge to the widow's pleas. In contrast to the judge who delays because of his venality or his indifference, God "will quickly grant justice to his chosen ones who cry out to him." Jesus says. He won't delay long in helping them like the unjust judge delayed helping the woman. God's help will come speedily. The emphasis is not on the negative picture of justice which the parable itself portrays, but rather on the contrast between the reluctance of the unjust judge and the willingness of God to act on behalf of those who cry out to him. If a corrupt and unjust judge will render justice because the plaintiff is so persistent, how much more is God, who loves us and is concerned about us, willing to answer us when we call to him?

In view of the parable's insistence that God will bring justice and bring it speedily, what then are we to make of our sense that God seems to be taking his own sweet time about fulfilling his promises to make things right? The parable suggests a two-fold answer: In the first place, our notion of when and how a problem ought to be solved does not necessarily correspond to God's solutions. That's why the widow can represent the human side of the experience of waiting for justice, but the judge does not represent God's response. God, however, does not operate by human time-clocks. God sees the end from the beginning, and he answers the cry of his people speedily, but speedily in relation to God's own knowledge of the situation and according to his own timetable. It is our impatience and our desire to have every problem solved immediately that leads us to experience the situation as justice delayed.

I heard a story which illustrates how we often confuse God's timing with ours. A country newspaper had been running a series of articles on the value of church attendance. One day, a letter to the editor was received in the newspaper office. It read, "Print this if you dare. I have been trying an experiment. I have a field of corn which I plowed on Sunday. I planted it on Sunday. I did all the cultivating on Sunday. I gathered the harvest on Sunday and hauled it to my barn on Sunday.

I find that my harvest this October is just as great as any of my neighbors' who went to church on Sunday. So where was God all this time?" The editor printed the letter, but added his reply at the bottom. "Your mistake was in thinking that God always settles his accounts in October." That's often our mistake as well, isn't it — thinking that God should act when and how we want him to act, according to our timetable rather than his. The fact that our vision is limited, finite, unable to see the end from the beginning, somehow escapes our mind. So we complain; we get frustrated; we accuse God of being indifferent to us; we do not live by faith.

In fact, it may be our actions or behavior that cause what we experience as delay or unfair treatment. God always takes human freedom seriously. God does not will the ancient feuds in Rwanda and Burundi, nor does he will the violence that they spawn. But he does will human beings to be free to make decisions, even if those decisions are motivated by evil or wrong desires. So while God is at work to bring about his ends, he is at work through human individuals and human agencies, despite the injustice that often characterizes human relationships, because God respects our freedom.

In the second place, it is not our part, while waiting in patience to complain or to sulk or to be passive, but to be faithful and persistent in prayer. This is why Jesus says that we ought always to pray and not to lose heart. It is not our part to set the terms of how justice will be meted out; our part is to be faithful in prayer and faithful in life, and our faithfulness will enable us to wait in patience for God to act, even though in our limited time frame, we may not see God's will accomplished like we would like to see it.

Such persistence in prayer is what faithfulness to God is all about. It means refusing to give in to appearances and continuing to trust God to act in his way and in his time. It may appear that God does not hear. It may appear that we are alone and without supernatural help. It may appear that injustice and evil are prevailing. But faith dares to go on praying, to grasp the reality that we cannot see and live by it. This is really what makes people of faith different from others. We are willing to live by what we cannot see, but which we believe to be real, rather than by what we can see, and which the world, or our culture, tells us is real. Only someone who believes in a reality that is unseen will persist in praying. Everybody prays, but many people only pray when they're in a jam and are desperate because they can't come up with any fast and efficient human solution.

If we do not experience the power of God in our lives, it is probably due more to our failure to pray persistently than it is to God's reluctance to answer. When we don't get the answer we expect when we expect it, the temptation is to stop praying and start asking why. That is not faith; it is not faithful living. And the end of our gospel drives this point home. For after affirming God's willingness to hear our prayers and vindicate his people, Jesus poses this very poignant question, "Nevertheless, when the Son of Man comes, will he find faith on earth?" The real question is not about God's faithfulness, but about ours. The message of Luke is that God is faithful; therefore, the way to experience God's faithfulness is for us to have faith in him, to live by faith in God, to persist in trusting God, even when appearances do not seem to support either his existence or his concern for us. The righteous person lives by faith.

"When the Son of Man comes, will he find faith on the earth?" That is the question this parable asks of each of us. Where is the point in your life at which you need to let go of your fears, your frustrations, your impatience, your anger, and sink down into patient trust in God's timing and in his way of working? There's a point like that in each of our lives, a point where we need to let go of our desire for speed and efficiency and just sit back and let God work in his way and in his time, all the while living faithfully and praying persistently.

Ordinary Time 30
Luke 18:9-14

The Good, The Bad, And The Justified

The famous actor Gregory Peck was once standing in line with a friend, waiting for a table in a crowded Los Angeles restaurant. They had been waiting for some time, the diners seemed to be taking their time eating and new tables weren't opening up very fast. They weren't even that close to the front of the line. Peck's friend became impatient, and he said to Gregory Peck, "Why don't you tell the maitre d' who you are?" Gregory Peck responded with great wisdom. "No," he said, "if you have to tell them who you are, then you aren't."

That's a lesson that the Pharisee in our gospel reading apparently had never learned. His prayer, if it can be called that, is largely an advertisement for himself. He's selling himself to God. Little wonder that Luke describes him in the way he does, "The Pharisee stood and prayed thus with himself." That's a very apt description, isn't it — he prayed *with himself*. He would have done better had he had Gregory Peck there to whisper in his ear that if he had to remind God who he was, then he wasn't.

The tax collector, on the other hand, didn't have to tell God who he was. He knew who he was and he knew that God knew who he was. His prayer is not an exercise in self-promotion, but a confession and a plea for mercy. He is not selling himself, but opening himself. And Jesus says, "It is this man who went home justified." To be justified means to be declared "not guilty." It means to be declared right. The tax collector is declared to be in the right relationship to God while the Pharisee, who is so certain of his own righteousness, is shown to be in the wrong relationship with God. He is not justified before the bar of God's justice which is the court of ultimate consequence.

We hasten to add, however, that this does not mean that the Pharisee was a bad person and the tax collector really a good person. There's no suggestion of that in this parable. The Pharisee was probably every bit as good and moral and generous as he claimed to be. When he gives that little speech about how he fasts and tithes and gives alms and prays frequently, he's not guilty of false advertising. There's no suggestion that he's a hypocrite — pretending to be something he isn't. In fact, the Pharisees enjoyed great respect among the people of Israel because of the high standards of their morality, their ethics, and their piety. Nor is there any suggestion that the tax collector was really a good guy at heart — something akin to the Hollywood version of the prostitute with the heart of gold or the thief who robs only from the rich in order to give to the poor. The tax collector was very likely every bit as bad as his reputation made him out to be. If he hadn't been crooked, he wouldn't have been a tax collector in the first place, for the Romans couldn't get honest people to be their lackeys. The only people who would serve as tax collectors were people who were interested in enriching themselves with little concern for how they did it. The contrast in the parable is not between the real, but hidden, goodness of the tax collector and the real, but hidden, hypocrisy of the Pharisee. Such a construction misses the point. If that were the case, it would not be at all hard to understand why it is the tax collector and not the Pharisee who is declared to be righteous and who goes home justified.

No, this parable is much more radical than that, and it is so because the gospel is radical. It goes to the root of the problem of human sinfulness and alienation from God. The gospel that Jesus proclaims in this parable is radical in at least three aspects: first, the parable tells us that God knows us as we really are; second, that God accepts us as we are; and third, that though God accepts us as we are, he never leaves us as we are.

The first of those three aspects of the gospel is familiar to us, though we may not live in awareness of it all the time. *God knows who we are.* We don't have to do a snow-job on God and sell ourselves to him. Like the line in the Christmas song about Santa Claus, "he knows if you've been bad or good," God knows us. But God's knowledge of us goes much deeper than that. He knows not only our actions, but our motives, our intentions, our deepest and most intimate secrets, he even knows what is in the depths of our unconscious minds. The psalmist said it well when he said, "While I was in my mother's womb, while I was being created in secret, behold, O Lord, you knew me altogether" (Psalm 139:13, 15).

Such knowledge can be a frightening thing if we operate on the "God rewards the good and punishes the bad" philosophy. If that is the way things work, then I'm in trouble, because I've got things inside me that I wouldn't want anyone else to know. There are parts of me that are too private, too painful, too intimate to share with anyone. So if I think that my acceptance by God depends on him not knowing about who I really am inside, then I'm lost. That's why the news that God knows exactly who I am, better than I know myself, is such a liberating piece of good news. I don't have to pretend. I am who God knows me to be. I don't have to be afraid of him finding out something I'm ashamed of, I don't have to close off part of my life to him; he knows me with a knowledge that is deep and wonderful and intimate and infinite. Paul reminds us that when our time comes to finally stand in God's presence our own knowledge will be full and complete: "One day," he says, "I shall know, even as I am fully known" (1 Corinthians 13:12). What a wonderful prospect! So if you've got something to hide, don't bother. God already knows more about you than you will ever know until that day when he grants you fullness of knowledge and that will be heaven.

But close on the heels of this truth, comes the next part. *God not only knows who I am, but he accepts me as I am.* I say this is radical because it goes right against the grain of the way most of us think. If something good happens to somebody we know, we say, "Well, you must be living right," meaning that their goodness has been rewarded. When something bad happens to us, we immediately begin to wonder what we've done to cause God to punish us. It is normal for us to think that God blesses those who are good and punishes those who are bad. That's the way we would do it if we were God, and we project our own ideas of justice and reward and punishment onto God. The only problem with that is that God doesn't quite fit our expectations of him. As Karl Barth, the great theologian, would say, "God is God." He is not an idol created in our image. God is God. God acts as *God* acts. And Jesus says in this parable that God is a God who justifies the ungodly. He declares sinners to be in right relation to himself. He declares them not guilty. By human standards of justice, this is positively scandalous. God justifies the ungodly? Why? Because they are ungodly? No! God hates their ungodliness. Then why does he justify them? Because they trust in him for their justification, and that is the right or righteous thing to do. To throw oneself on the mercy of God is the right thing to do and God declares us righteous when we do it. That is the meaning of having faith or believing — having faith in God, believing that God will act like God and have mercy on us. The problem most of us have is that we don't act like God, and therefore, we are scandalized when God acts like God.

Samuel Colgate, the founder of the Colgate business empire, was a devout Christian, and he told of an incident that took place in the church he attended. During an evangelistic service, an invitation was given at the close of the homily for all those who wished to turn their lives over to Christ and be forgiven. One of the first persons to walk down the aisle and kneel at the altar was a well-known prostitute. She knelt in very real repentance, she wept, she asked God to forgive her, and meanwhile the rest of the congregation looked on approvingly at what she was doing. Then she stood and testified that she believed God had forgiven her for her past life, and she now wanted to become a member of the church. For a few moments, the silence was deafening. Finally, Samuel Colgate arose and said, "I guess we blundered when we prayed that the Lord would save sinners. We forgot to specify what kind of sinners. We'd better ask him to forgive us for this oversight. The Holy Spirit has touched this woman and made her truly repentant, but the Lord apparently doesn't understand that she's not the type we want him to rescue. We'd better spell it out for him just which sinners we had in mind." Immediately, a motion was made and unanimously approved that the woman be accepted into membership in the congregation.

God accepts us as we are. There's not a sin too black, not a deed too awful, not a thought too horrible for him to forgive. What cuts us off from his forgiveness and the freedom such forgiveness brings is our thinking that we have to justify ourselves. Trusting in our own righteousness does not bring God's verdict of not guilty. Trusting in God's righteousness does.

But if we say that God justifies the ungodly, doesn't that appear to condone bad or sinful behavior? If God doesn't require us to change before he accepts us, then what's the use of being good at all? Why not sin boldly and have a good time? After all, the scriptures say that there is pleasure in sin, for a time. Ah, but here the third truth comes into play. God knows who we are; he accepts us as we are; *but he never leaves us as we are.* When God justifies us on the basis of our faith in him, he also transforms us and makes us better than we are.

The theological or biblical term for God's forgiving and claiming work in us is justification. The word for God's cleansing and purifying within us is sanctification. God starts with us just where he find us, whether in the palace or the pig sty, but he never leaves us there. For God's purpose is not just to rescue us from hell but to get us ready for heaven. So he's in the business of making us holy, or to put it as the writer of Ephesians 4:15 does, helping us "to grow up in every way into Christ who is our head." Maturity in Christ, spiritual adulthood, perfection in love — these are all ways to describe God's work in our lives subsequent to the moment when he justifies us, or declares us righteous.

This sanctifying work of God's spirit within us, does not turn us into stained-glass saints, people who walk around piously with their hands folded in prayer all day. God's work within us is the most practical, down-to-earth (or perhaps we should say up-to-heaven) work imaginable. When we open our lives to his gracious presence, when we no longer trust in our own morality or good behavior or willpower, we find the most amazing things beginning to happen. As we experience more of God's love for us, we find ourselves becoming more loving toward others. People with bad tempers find that God's spirit within them enables them to control their temper. People with enslaving habits like alcoholism or addiction to gambling, find a resource that is beyond themselves and a source of strength to overcome those diseases of the soul. People with too much love of money and material things find that their values begin to change. People with deep insecurities and low self-esteem begin to see themselves and love themselves as God loves them and sees them.

This doesn't all happen at once, of course. Discipleship, sanctification, spiritual maturity, whatever you want to call it, is a life-long process. It's a journey. We don't become saints overnight, but we do *become*. That's the nature of the Christian life — becoming conformed to the image of Christ.

The transforming work of the Holy Spirit in the life of a believer was the chief theme of John Wesley's life and work, and a distinctive contribution the Methodists make to the rest of the church. Wesley had a four-fold dictum: "All people need to be saved from sin; all people can be saved from sin; all people can know they are saved from sin; and all people can be saved to the uttermost." It is that latter that Wesley particularly emphasized. He called it "going on to perfection." He didn't mean a sinless kind of moral perfection, not a perfection in knowledge, but a perfection in love. The single identifying mark of the Holy Spirit's work in our lives is love. Do we love God and do we love one another? That's the test of our sanctification.

Wesley was always deeply disturbed when he saw Christians who were more like the Pharisee than the tax collector — people who trusted in their own righteousness, and consequently, showed little evidence of the growing presence of God's love in their lives. Once while he was preaching, he noticed a lady in the congregation who was known for her critical attitudes toward others. All through the service she stared at his tie, with a frown on her face. At the end of the service, she came up to him and said very sharply, "Mr. Wesley, the strings on your bow tie are much too long. It offends me." Wesley immediately asked for a pair of scissors, and when someone handed them to him, he gave them to the woman and said, "Then by all means, trim it to your satisfaction." She did so, clipping off an inch or so from each side. "Are you sure they're all right now," he asked, and she replied, "Yes, that's much better."

"Then let me have the scissors for a moment," Wesley said, "for I'm sure you won't mind a bit of correction either. I do not wish to be cruel, madam, but your tongue offends me — it is too long. Please stick it out so that I may trim some of it off." Needless to say, this critic got the point.

Now God may not take a pair of scissors to our tongue, but for some of us, that may be the part of us where he chooses to begin his sanctifying work, for it is one of the things by which we give most offense and sin against love. But whether it's our tongue or our ambition or our lust or our prejudice or our materialism or our pride or our self-righteousness, or whatever else our besetting sin may be, God will not be content until Christ's image is perfectly formed in us, and that is why he will never leave us as he finds us. Like a dentist who will insist on pulling the tooth with the abscess in it, rather than merely giving us some pain-killer, God will insist on removing the abscesses from our souls. We do not have to remove them to make ourselves acceptable to him; he accepts us warts and all, as the saying goes. But he will insist on giving us the full treatment, causing us a lesser pain in order to spare us an infinitely greater one — the pain of a life without him.

What aspect of the gospel speaks most to your needs? Is it the fact that God knows you, and knows you intimately and fully? If so, then accept the freedom that God offers you. Open yourself to him, confess who you are to him, and you will find him gracious. Perhaps it is the second aspect which speaks most keenly to you — that God accepts you as you are and declares us righteous on the basis of your trust in him. That too is liberating. Not only do you not have to hide your real self, but you do not have to make yourself good. Accept his love. Accept his forgiveness which he offers you in Christ. Accept his claim upon you. Accept your adoption into the family of God. Or maybe you've experienced that much of the gospel — the knowledge that you are loved and accepted and justified — but you have not experienced the transforming work of the Spirit in your life, because you have not understood or because you have not been open to allow him to work. If so, then open yourself to the Spirit as fully as you are consciously capable of doing; give him the freedom to cleanse away all that is incompatible with the love of Christ, accept his discipline, commit yourself to "going in for the full treatment." This, too, is a work of faith, a matter of trust, for we do not make ourselves holy. It is God who makes us like Christ. We will not have better morals or better ethics or more willpower when we decide to. We will have them when we allow God to change our inner nature into conformity with the nature of Christ. When Christ is formed in us, then we will be better people with better behavior. So our salvation from God's knowledge of us in our mother's wombs to our perfected knowledge of ourselves and of him in heaven is the work of his grace and the product of faith. From beginning to end, we are saved by God's grace.

Ordinary Time 31
Luke 19:1-10

Out On
A Limb

    A friend told me of the hours he spent as a child in a large cherry tree in his grandmother's backyard. The tree was very large and high, at least as he remembered it. He remembered the very first time he climbed it. He had to jump to catch hold of the lowest branch, and then pull himself by sheer muscle power up onto it. Then he could work his way up the tree. The tree seemed so high, that he got dizzy looking down, and yet, scary as it was, he couldn't resist climbing higher and higher. Finally he got very close to the top where the branches were thinner, and he could climb no higher. He stayed there, straddling a limb and holding tightly to one above it, swaying in the breeze with the leaves fluttering around him. It was an exhilarating moment for a seven-year-old. He was on top of the world.
    But when the time came to climb back down, he was terrified. As long as he was on his way up, his vision and his focus was on the branch above him. But on the way down, all he could see was how far below the ground was and how many protruding limbs there were between him and the ground. Very gingerly, he made his way down, branch by branch, and when he finally got on the ground, he discovered his knees were trembling with the excitement and fear of the whole experience. Like a typical small boy, however, once he knew he could

conquer the tree, he couldn't stay out of it, and before long, he went up and down it like a monkey. Somehow, the risk of being out on a limb high in the tree became as routine as brushing one's teeth.

Years later, long after he had grown out of his tree-climbing days, he was visiting his grandparents and happened to notice the old cherry tree. The lower limb that had been his first step up into the tree, the limb that he had had to leap to catch hold of, now was at shoulder height. The whole tree seemed somehow shrunken and unprepossessing. It wasn't nearly as large as he remembered it. The thin branches near the top, where he had spent many a summer hour swaying in the breezes and feeling himself to be on top of the world, were no more than 20 feet from the ground. He laughed as he saw the tree through the adult eyes, but he remembered and relived for a few moments, his feelings as that seven-year-old boy with trembling knees taking a daring risk to climb up among the clouds.

The gospel is about another tree-climber whose name was Zacchaeus. He too experienced the risk and exhilaration of being "out on a limb." Zacchaeus' life was transformed as he sat on his tree limb, and at the time, it must have been a thoroughly scary experience, though perhaps later, as a mature disciple, he may have wondered why it ever seemed risky or frightening at all.

Luke, alone, tells us this story. He places it in the context of his account of Jesus' journey to Jerusalem. Following Mark's gospel, one of his main sources, he relates the story of Jesus' healing of a blind man near the city of Jericho. But then he adds this story about Jesus' encounter with a man named Zacchaeus.

Jesus is just passing through Jericho, Luke tells us. He apparently didn't have any pressing engagements there. He wasn't contemplating a preaching mission or healings. He was just passing through. He was going to Jerusalem. Jerusalem was the focus of his vision at this point. He had a rendezvous with destiny, and nothing would deter him from keeping it. So Jericho is just a way station, a place one had to go through to get to Jerusalem. Yet, it becomes the place of a significant encounter.

This is often the case, isn't it? The places and situations that we consider temporary or simply way stations turn out to be the places or situations that hold the most significance for us. Henri Nouwen once said something to the effect that in his ministry he found himself becoming frustrated and resentful that his work was constantly being interrupted by people who wanted or needed something from him, until one day the Lord spoke to him and revealed that his real work was in those interruptions. So I think we have to pay attention to the transit points on our journey. It just may be that we'll discover someone, perhaps even ourselves, who is out on a limb and needs some attention.

If Jericho did not figure prominently in Jesus' plans, however, Jesus' transit through Jericho certainly loomed large in Zacchaeus' mind, as well as in the mind of other citizens of the town. We're only told two facts about Zacchaeus: he was the chief tax collector, and he was short. Whether there was any relationship between those two facts, we don't know. Luke has not delved into Zacchaeus' psychological makeup, so we don't have any basis for addressing that question. But those two facts do figure prominently in the story.

As chief tax collector, Zacchaeus was a traitor to his people and nation. He was a collaborator and agent of the imperialist Romans who had imposed their rule on Palestine by military conquest and occupation. At a time when zealot movements were springing up to oppose Roman rule through guerilla warfare, tax collectors were the pariahs of society. Zacchaeus may have seen himself as a practitioner of "realpolitik," but his countrymen saw him as a thief and a traitor. I say thief, because though Rome required a certain amount in taxes from its colonial subjects, it also turned a blind eye to how much the tax collector was able to gouge for his own pockets above and beyond the required sum. So long as he was not so greedy that he incited actual revolt, he was free to fleece his fellow-citizens for as much as he could get them to cough up. So Zacchaeus was not exactly the most popular fellow in Jericho, though undoubtedly he was one of the best-known. And certainly, he would never need fear that people were indifferent to him.

The other fact also is important — that he was short. For it is this fact that moves the action in the story. His shortness of stature prevents him from seeing over the people lining the street to catch a glimpse of Jesus and his company as they pass through Jericho. Everybody loves a parade, and no excuse is too trivial. So the townspeople are out to see this man whose reputation has preceded him from Galilee where he has spent most of his life and ministry. They're not about to make way for this shrimp of a tax collector.

So Zacchaeus is forced to do something he probably hasn't done since he was a boy. He climbs a tree. Apparently he hasn't lost his tree-climbing skills from when he was a small boy. Actually, climbing a tree is like riding a bike; once you learn you never really forget how to do it. Your joints may be less flexible and more creaky, but you still know how to do it. So Zacchaeus gets up into the tree, and eases his way out onto a limb so he will have a good view of Jesus when he passes by. (I can imagine the remarks that others are making when they see this, and the crude attempts at humor that compare Zacchaeus to his ancestors the apes.)

When Jesus comes along, he stops beneath the tree and says, "Zacchaeus, hurry and come down; for I must stay at your house today." And Luke says, "So he hurried down and was happy to welcome him." Wait a minute. Hasn't Luke left out a lot here? He hasn't told us how Jesus knew Zacchaeus' name, nor even intimated that Zacchaeus must have nearly fallen out of his tree when he heard himself being addressed by this Galilean rabbi he's heard about, but never laid eyes on before. We're left to wonder about the details. Did Zacchaeus flatter himself by thinking that his own reputation had spread to Galilee, so that his name was a household word? Was he stricken with a sense of awe and dread that a total stranger should come right to where he was hanging out on a limb and stop and call him by name? Had somebody ratted on him to Jesus to cause trouble for him? We don't know. All this is left to our imaginations. The story itself is laconic and spare. Jesus calls; Zacchaeus responds. Just like that.

We're not left to imagine the reaction of the other people standing around, however. They are clearly unhappy. Here they are, all good, law-abiding, patriotic citizens who know whom to despise and whom to approve. Jesus' attentions to Zacchaeus are not appreciated at all by the other onlookers. Why should he single out Zacchaeus to provide the honor of hospitality rather than some of them who remain steadfast in their hatred of the Romans and in their support of nationalistic aspirations? Why go stay in the home of a sinner? It's one thing to love sinners in the abstract; it's another to sleep in their houses. In the Middle East, even today, providing hospitality to others is considered a great honor and solemn duty. It's hard for us to grasp the real import of what is happening here. For us, playing the host is sometimes seen as a duty that has to be performed, but we're always glad when our guests go away and we get the house back to ourselves. But Jesus, by inviting Zacchaeus to provide him with hospitality is paying Zacchaeus honor and respect. He is, quite literally, gracing Zacchaeus with his presence.

But if Zacchaeus was "out on a limb" in the literal sense, he's even more "out on a limb" when he stands before Jesus. Jesus' invitation to come down out of his tree, and his unexpected and gracious offer to come stay in his house calls forth from Zacchaeus a similarly unexpected and grace-filled response. It's a response that is far more risky and scary than his climb up into the branches of the tree ever was. "Lord, half of my possessions I will give to the poor, and if I have defrauded anyone of anything, I will pay back four times as much." Now that's what I call conversion!

Jesus has not demanded anything of Zacchaeus. Rather he has offered him the opportunity to play the magnanimous host, giving Zacchaeus stature far beyond his natural height.

Yet this offer of grace, for that's what it is, calls forth a willingness on Zacchaeus' part to respond in kind. Jesus hasn't censured him for being a tax collector. He hasn't said a word about his sinful gouging of his fellow citizens to enrich his own coffers. He hasn't breathed the word "traitor." He's just announced his intention to stay with Zacchaeus. And yet that offer presents Zacchaeus with a demand that is far more fraught with risk than anything he has ever done or dreamed of doing. Or perhaps, he has dreamed of doing it. Perhaps that's where this blurted out promise of generosity comes from — from Zacchaeus' dreams of being a better person than he is. As he stands before Jesus, perhaps he sees himself, not as he is, a morally-stunted and hated tax collector, but as the benefactor of the poor and the righter of wrongs that he may become.

That's really being "out on a limb," isn't it — to see ourselves as we might become, and to commit ourselves to begin living by that vision rather than by what we think of ourselves or what others think of us? It's a scary risk to catch a vision of what we might become with the help of grace. It's risky to let go of our comfort zones, our status quo, our familiar sins, our cherished self-images, and stand before Jesus exposed for what we are, and exposed to what we may become.

I suggest to you that the encounter with the living Christ produces just that effect in us. We see ourselves in a light we never saw ourselves in before. We see that we are as unworthy and sinful as we admit in the privacy of our own hearts, and that we may become better and more useful than we hardly dared to dream. I am not offering a psychologizing version of personal transformation here. This encounter with the living Christ which calls forth from us qualities of character and behavior we never knew or allowed, but perhaps always hoped, we had, is nothing less than a miracle of grace. It is, in fact, what salvation is all about. When Jesus says, "Today salvation has come to this house," he is responding to this "blurted out" new self that Zacchaeus has just discovered — this self that is concerned about justice and restitution. Salvation is becoming who we really are in Christ, and then living that new self out in concrete ways that manifest God's redeeming work in the world.

The crowd of good people who grumbled at grace that day don't seem to have profited by their encounter with Jesus. It is they who hear Jesus' reminder that the Son of Man came to seek and to save the lost. For those who grumble at grace never experience it. Those who risk accepting it discover that their lives are changed forever. So salvation came to Zacchaeus because he was willing to go out on a limb to see Jesus. And salvation comes to us when we are willing to go out on a limb and risk becoming all that we can be through the grace of that same Jesus Christ.

Feast Of All Saints
Matthew 5:1-12
Revelation 7:2-4, 9-14

Remembering The Saints

There was a column in the *New York Times* on Wednesday, October 28, 1992, by Robertson Davies titled "Haunted By Halloween." After tracing the origins of Halloween to the ancient Celtic festival of the Death of the Year, and showing how the Christian church piggybacked the Feast of All Saints onto this pagan festival which marked both the death of the sun at the beginning of winter and the remembrance of their dead ancestors, Davies argued for a recovery of the best part of the ancient Halloween — the remembrance of the dead.

> *Let us recognize that we are not the ultimate triumph but rather that we are beads on a string. Let us behave with decency to the beads that were strung before us, and hope modestly that the beads that come after us will not hold us of no account because we are dead ... What might we profitably do on Halloween? Look backward, and consider those who went before us. The road ahead is inevitably dark, but to see where we have been may offer unexpected hints about who we are and where we should be heading. Triviality about the past leads certainly toward a trivial future.*

John Wesley, the 18th century founder of Methodism, said that the Feast of All Saints was his favorite festival in the church year. It was the one time, more than at any other, when the great chain of witness, from the earliest worshippers of the God of Abraham, Isaac and Jacob, was emphasized and brought into the present through remembrance. I think it's my favorite too. On All Saints, more than at any other time, I feel surrounded by a great cloud of witnesses.

That wonderful, magnificent passage from the Book of Revelation which is our epistle, and which some of us can never hear without wanting to sing it as Handel set it to music in *The Messiah,* is a passage of remembrance of the heroic witnesses to the faith. Psychologists tell us that our memories are what form our sense of identity. Events and persons which do not stick in our memories really do not influence us much at all. The things and persons we remember, however, have the power to shape us and mold us and direct us long after they are past and gone, even when those memories are deeply buried in our subconscious mind. To a large extent, we are what we remember. I don't mean primarily the kind of remembering that we do when we're cramming for an exam, and we try to make dates and times and equations stick in our heads long enough to regurgitate them for the professor, or the kind of remembering we do when our husband or wife says, "Honey, don't forget to stop for milk on your way home." I'm speaking of remembering in a much deeper sense.

A Methodist pastor had lunch with an Episcopal priest with whom he had gone to college 25 years earlier, and whom he hadn't seen or kept in touch with all those years. They didn't talk about anything serious; they just remembered together. Through their memories, they relived their college days, names of significant people came up, and with their names came faces and voices and a reaffirmation of what those people had meant to them for good or for ill. And with that remembrance of things past came a deeper level of understanding of who they were now, compared with who they had been back then. We've probably all had similar experiences. And the strange thing is that when we do this kind of significant remembering of the persons in the past who have had important influences on us, we begin to get a sense of our place in the world, and a hint or a glimpse of where we might be headed. In short, memory leads to hope.

And that's what's happening in this passage from the Revelation. The seer is writing to seven congregations in Asia Minor somewhere near the end of the first century and the beginning of the second. In the 50 or 60 years since Jesus was crucified, the new movement of people who believed that he had been raised from death had spread significantly over the whole Roman Empire, as far west as Gaul, or what is now France and Spain. Christians made up a significant block of the population and were recognized as (potentially at least) a powerful political force. This made the emperor Domitian a bit edgy, and to make sure he was able to hold the empire together, large and unwieldy as it was, he instituted a kind of pledge of allegiance, similar in intent to our own pledge of allegiance to the flag, but with more serious repercussions. In Domitian's version, however, subject people as well as Roman citizens were required to offer, once a year in one of the temples of the state religion, a sacrifice to the divine genius of the emperor. Failure to do so constituted treason, and was punishable by imprisonment, exile, or even death. Domitian didn't really believe he was divine; the doctrine of the emperor's divinity was a political doctrine. If the emperor was descended from the gods, then his rule was legitimized.

And since most of the Christians were cosmopolitan peoples of the Graeco-Roman world, the emperor figured he could ensure their loyalty by making them say the pledge of allegiance. Was he ever in for a surprise! First of all, he discovered, they were as devoted to the worship of their God Christus as the Jews ever were to theirs. But when they were threatened with exile or even death for refusing to take the oath of loyalty, they reacted in a very surprising way. They didn't revolt or use their numbers to create political instability by preaching insurrection. Instead, they willingly walked to the stake to be burned, or into the arenas where the lions waited, singing praises to their God and speaking words of forgiveness to their persecutors. They became martyrs.

The word "martyr" literally means witness. Their witness to their faith in Christ was so strong, so potent, that they willingly went to their deaths rather than compromise with a state which they believed was making illegitimate demands upon them.

And so, to these Christians who were living through a time of great ordeal, John, one of their pastors who had been exiled to a penal colony in the Aegean Sea, wrote this visionary letter to them. By adopting this visionary style of literature, he invites them to use their imaginations to glimpse a different reality above and beyond the grim time of testing which confronts them on an almost daily basis. He lets them see what's really going on, if only they could eavesdrop on God holding court in heaven. As they feel the flames begin to lick around their feet at the stake, or hear the roars of the hungry lions, they can take hope that above and behind and within this terrible ordeal, there is a different reality. He calls to their remembrance the example of faithful people who have witnessed to their faith in God without flinching, and he turns their eyes toward the future when they will be part of that great innumerable throng from every nation, tribe and the language, who stand around the throne of God singing "Blessing and glory and wisdom and thanks and honor and power and might be to our God forever and ever!" The memory of past faithful ones will inspire them to faithfulness in their own time of ordeal and cement the bond which binds the whole people of God, past, present, and future, into one vast and thrilling community of worship. And this remembrance will renew and strengthen them in hope.

Robertson Davies was right about our need to remember our dead — those who have gone before us. What sense of family solidarity can we have if we do not remember our fathers and mothers, our grandparents and great-grandparents who have made such an impact on our lives? And if it is so important to our sense of identity to remember our biological families, how vital is it also that we remember our ancestors in faith? How can we hope to know how our faith relates to the present circumstances we face if we know nothing of how that faith gave hope and meaning to others who have gone before us? We Americans, perhaps more so than any other people on earth, lack a strong and vital historical memory. We live totally in the present divorced from the past and with little hope in the future. We don't remember, and so we cannot understand who we are and where we are going or what we are becoming.

And this American penchant for loss of memory creeps over into our churches and religious life as well. We ignore, actually devalue, what generations of Christians have learned about God before us. We are ignorant of theology, ignorant of the great tradition of spirituality and worship which has preceded us, content often to live only for the spiritual impulses of the moment. We don't know that we stand upon the shoulders of giants, and that if we can see any glimpse of God at all, it is only because there have been faithful witnesses who have helped us see, and who are now part of that great throng singing praises to the Lamb who is in the center of the throne of God.

These giants of faith upon whose shoulders we stand are not necessarily those whom the world would acknowledge as giants. A few are Paul, whose grasp of the mind of Christ has never been equalled; Augustine; Thomas Aquinas; Theresa of Avila; Lady Julian of Norwich; Martin Luther; John Wesley and his faithful mother Susanna; the saintly Japanese Christian Kagawa or Mother Teresa of Calcutta — these and a relatively few others have attracted notice beyond their immediate circumstances and helped shape the faith of thousands or even millions.

But most of the giants of faith have been people, who for the most part were unheralded and unknown, except to those whose lives they personally touched and to whom they gave hope. They are those quiet saints who have visibly manifested the qualities Jesus pronounced blessed in the Beatitudes —

poverty of spirit, humility, purity of heart, mercy, hunger for justice, and peacemakers.

Today is a day for remembering the faithful witnesses in our own spiritual family tree. A friend told me of the influence of his great-grandmother, whom he doubted he would find it very easy to really like if she were still alive. She was the epitome of a dour, ultra-strict Scots-Irish Protestant who didn't have the greatest sense of humor in the world. But she did have a passionate love for God and a wonderful and powerful life of prayer. One of my friend's earliest memories is from the time when he was about three or four years old, his parents were away and he was sleeping at Great-grandma's house. He remembers waking up frightened in the middle of the night because it was dark and he could hear voices. But he discovered it was Gram, down on her knees beside the bed praying fervently for some missionary that her church supported. In the morning, she told him that God had awakened her from sleep and told her to pray for such and such a missionary. And she said that this happened very often. When he asked how God spoke to her, she just said that the thought came clearly into her mind, and she just knew she was supposed to pray. So pray she did. And as my friend grew older, he understood that this was just a normal part of his great-grandmother's life. She probably spent more time in the middle of the night on her knees than in bed asleep. But letters would come from missionaries all over the world, telling of some experience where they were in need or in trouble, and were assured by that same inner voice that she was praying for them, and it gave them courage and hope. Her example of intercessory prayer inspired her daughter-in-law to similarly pray for not only the missionaries, but for each of her children and grandchildren every day of her life, and her granddaughter still never lets a day go without spending some significant time on her knees in prayer for her three sons who are pastors and for all her nephews and nieces and cousins who are in ministry.

Today is a day for all of us to remember the saints, all the saints who have trod the path of faithfulness to God before us, and especially those whom we have personally encountered on our journey, whose witness to their faith has contributed so much to our own. When we gather around the Lord's table, we gather to remember in this deep sense: we eat and drink the bread and wine in remembrance of Jesus. And by remembering, we recall his life into ours to help us know who we are and what the meaning of our journey is, and we learn to trust him to lead us into the future. But we don't gather alone; we are part of the communion of saints. And those words that we say at the beginning of the Great Thanksgiving as we gather around the Lord's table, ring in our hearts with new meaning, "And so, with your people on earth, and all the company of heaven we praise your name, and join their unending hymn . . . ." That's who we're in fellowship with this morning — all the saints in earth and heaven, who by their faithful witness to Jesus Christ, offer us the priceless gift of hope.

Ordinary Time 32
Luke 20:27-38

The Importance Of Asking The Right Questions

A clergy colleague has made it a policy for many years to refer what he calls "six-year-old theology questions" to his wife. Since she has taught very young children for many years, she has a much better grasp than he does of how to address the real concerns in questions which little kids ask. The other day, a first-grader brought a picture with him into her class where she teaches English as a second language. He had found it in the trash basket in another class. It was a drawing of a skeleton, titled "Inside of Me." It was designed to teach children that everyone has a skeleton inside of them. He unfolded it proudly and showed it to the class. One little girl from India was astounded at the thought that she and others had this scary-looking skeleton inside them, and so she pressed the issue a bit farther. "Even you got one of these inside you, Mrs. K?" The teacher replied, "Yes, I have one too." The next question was the theological one. "Even God got one inside him?" Now in a class made up of children from many different countries, cultures, and religious backgrounds (most of them not Christians), you can imagine that this question had the potential for major theological debate. I doubt if I'd have had the presence of mind to give the answer my friend's wife did; but, as usual, her expertise in six-year-old theology saved the day. "If God needs a skeleton, I'm sure he has one," she replied.

"God has everything he needs." This apparently satisfied the theological curiosity of the class, and they got on with the lesson.

Asking questions is an essential part of learning. If we don't know something, we look for someone who does and we ask. The only dumb question is the one you don't ask because you think it's a dumb question. We learn by asking questions about what we don't know.

While no question is a dumb question if it is designed to help you acquire knowledge or information which you don't currently have, there are questions which are the wrong questions to ask, and which, if asked, will actually prevent us from learning what we need to know.

We see two examples of these kinds of questions in our scripture passages. In the prophecy of Zechariah, we're told that the people came to the prophet to ask a question. About 50 years earlier, in 587 B.C., the Babylonian empire had conquered Judea, destroying Jerusalem and the temple of God. The leading citizens were then carried off into exile. For the people who remained in the land of Palestine during the 70 years before the Exiles came back, the memory of the devastation of their holy city and the temple of God was a powerful political force uniting the people. Since the temple had been destroyed in the fifth month of the year and the governor of Jerusalem executed in the seventh month, every year thereafter, the people fasted and mourned during the fifth and seventh months. In this way, they based their lives on the memory of the destruction they had suffered in the past.

The question that the people come to the prophets to ask is this, "Now that 50 or so years have passed, and the Babylonians have been defeated by the Persians, should we continue to fast and mourn in the fifth and seventh months?" Now that sounds like a harmless enough question, doesn't it? They're a little confused by the change of administrations, and they're not quite sure of how to proceed. Change the words "Bablyonian" and "Persian" to "Republicans" and "Democrats," and suddenly the question seems surprisingly contemporary.

But the answer they get from the prophet is not the answer they were expecting.

The answer to their question is itself a question — from God! "Then the word of the Lord of hosts came to me: Say to all the people of the land and the priests: When you fasted and lamented in the fifth month and in the seventh, was it for me that you fasted? And when you eat and when you drink, do you not eat and drink only for yourselves?" (Zechariah 7:4-7).

Their question is a self-serving question. It does not arise out of a desire to know the truth, to gain knowledge of God's will, but out of a desire to get God's sanction on their own national pity-party. They want God to bless their long-nurtured resentments, to sanction their long-standing hatred of those who destroyed their temple and holy city. Every year, when they fast on the fifth and seventh months, they are, in effect, saying, "This is who we are: We're the people who were beaten up by the Babylonians. Now this new administration had come, and we're not sure we want to change. We've grown comfortable with our identity; we like our fasts and our mourning and our moaning about the good old days. Can't we keep on doing this?"

But God let them know in no uncertain terms that they had asked the wrong question. "Was it for me you fasted? No, you did it for yourselves. Your concern was not with what I require of you, but with your own agenda. Your religion is a religion designed to make yourself feel better, not a religion designed to please God and enable you to do what God requires. And then comes God's pointed commands about the sort of religion he's really interested in: "Render true judgments, show kindness and mercy to one another; do not oppress the widow, the orphan, the alien, or the poor; and do not devise evil in your hearts against one another" (Zechariah 7:9-10). The clear implication is that while they piously fasted and mourned to commemorate the oppression and injustice which they suffered at the hands of a foreign nation, they themselves practiced oppression within their own nation against all those who were without power or an advocate.

When we ask the wrong question, in this case, a self-serving question, we shouldn't be surprised if we get an answer that we neither expect nor wish to hear. Our question becomes a judgment upon us. Like the people of ancient Judea, if we are going to find our way forward as a nation, we are going to have to stop asking questions that serve only our own individual or parochial interests and start asking the larger questions about truth, justice, kindness, mercy, and meeting needs that may be more pressing than our own.

In God's world, there is no true security for those who are unwilling to risk themselves and their own comfort for the sake of kindness, mercy, justice, and truth. All such comfort is false comfort. It is the comfort of the dead. Real life is life on the edge, always at risk, always vulnerable, always demanding that we live by faith and not by sight. That we live by trust in God rather than trust in our bank account. That we live by hope rather than by achievement. That we live for others rather than for ourselves.

The Sadducees who came to Jesus brought a similar kind of question. Their question is an attack question. It's a question designed to destroy the other person's viewpoint so that one's own viewpoint wins without ever having to be defended. Its purpose, like the other, is to prevent them from having to change. The Sadducees weren't really interested in what Jesus believed about the possibility of resurrection from the dead. Their question about one bride for seven brothers was not a question which they hoped would bring them some new knowledge or understanding. They already knew that the law which obligated a man to marry his brother's widow and raise up children by her which would legally be his dead brother's children was a compassionate social custom designed to provide for people who had no voice or standing in that culture — widows — and to ensure the continuity of a family's line. They didn't need to be instructed on the meaning and significance of levirate marriage. Their question was not serious, except that it was seriously designed to entrap Jesus into taking a position that would alienate people while making themselves look good at his expense.

We're familiar with questions like that, aren't we? We've all used these sorts of questions from time to time, haven't we — the question designed not to bring us closer to the truth, but to demolish the other person's point of view so that we protect ourselves from having to change our own behavior or cherished ideas.

But Jesus' opponents are the ones who are demolished by their own questions. He cuts through to the real issue — do they really believe in God? Is their God big enough and powerful enough to raise the dead? His God is. The God of Abraham, Isaac, and Jacob is. God is a God of the living. And people of faith, whether long dead or not, are alive to this God, who is the author not of death but of life.

This business of learning to ask the right questions applies not only to our national life, but to every area of life. It applies to our life as a church, certainly. If we are always asking the question, "What should we do so that we will not have to give up the things we've become comfortable doing?" we will never become what God wants us to be and we will not experience the very security we seek.

At a church-growth workshop the leader, Bill Easum, who himself grew a church from 29 members to over 2,400 members, said that too often the questions churches ask themselves are questions that are motivated by a desire to maintain whatever is comfortable. That's why some wag has said that the seven last words of the church are "We've never done it that way before." Bill Easum spoke of the three greatest sins of the church, and one of them was, "We're more in love with our traditions than we are with our missions." If we are intent on preserving the patterns of church life we've grown comfortable with, we'll soon discover that God has moved on and left us behind. God is always out there ahead of us, leading us into the future, and if we want to be working hand in hand with God, we have to be willing to ask the right questions. Not, "What can we do to preserve what we find comfortable?" but "What can we do to be partners with God in mission?" The first question leads to a church that is dead and declining; the second to a church that is alive and dynamic.

The same is true in our personal lives as well. How often we settle for what's comfortable instead of what is true and life-giving. It takes no effort, demands no sacrifice, involves no risk to simply go along with what the world says is important at any moment. It takes no courage, no commitment, no faith to just go on doing what we've been doing. To go on working 60- and 70-hour weeks to provide for our family's material comfort, and watch our families go down the drain because we're too busy working to be present for them. It's easier even to live with our addictions and compulsions than it is to confront and overcome them. Healing is hard work, and frequently, it is very painful work as well. Yet without the willingness to get out of the comfort zone, healing cannot come.

The poet T. S. Eliot in his famous poem "The Wasteland," calls April the "cruelest month," because the showers of April stir up the dull and dormant roots of trees and flowers to begin bursting forth with new life instead of allowing them to remain comfortably asleep in the frozen ground of winter. Yet the sleep of tree roots and flower bulbs is the sleep of hibernation, not of rest. Trees were meant to put out green leaves; tulips were meant to push up through the soil and produce beautiful blossoms. Human beings are also meant to grow, to mature, to blossom, not to hibernate in the frozen sleep of habit or tradition or familiarity. Paul says that we were meant to grow until "we attain to the full height of the stature of Christ."

And that's often the point of our fear. We're more afraid of change, more afraid of growth, than we are of becoming stuck in our present level of development. Better a comfortable rut than the risks of the journey. Yet God is a God of the living, not of the dead. God is always there nudging us to get out of our ruts, to leave false comfort and security behind, and take the risks of faith by following him into the future. The future is only frightening if God is not there ahead of us. If God is there, then what do we have to fear? What looks from our angle like a risky business — growing, moving on, living by faith rather than by sight — from another angle is the safest of all possible places to be, in God's company.

At every level of life, our personal life where we seek fulfillment and meaning, our life as a church seeking to be faithful in our mission, and our life as a nation seeking to move into the future, we must ask the right questions if we're going to discover something more than the false comfort of the status quo, if we're going to discover where God is actively stirring dull roots into new life. We must learn to ask not, "What should we do so that we can be most comfortable, so that we will not have to be changed?" but "Where must we go, what must we do, to find our true life in God?"

Ordinary Time 33
Luke 21:5-19

Not Yet
Quitting Time

You may remember reading or hearing of the Korean Christian group who predicted that Christ was going to return on October 28, 1992, all Christians would be taken to heaven, and the rest of the world would enter the terrible catastrophes of the end times. Well, we're still here, and unless you count the presidential election which was held a month later as a terrible apocalyptic catastrophe, I don't see that the ordinary catastrophes were much worse than usual.

There's nothing new in this miscalculation of what we have come to call the second coming or the second advent of Christ. For centuries, Christians, especially those who belong to sectarian groups, have been attempting to use the scriptures to calculate the timing of the second coming, and always without success. This practice began extremely early. Even within our New Testament, for example in Paul's first letter to the Thessalonians, which was written only about ten years after Jesus' crucifixion, we see an attempt to come to terms with this expectation. Almost from the moment the earliest Christians became convinced that Jesus had been raised from the dead by the power of God, they began looking for him to return to earth in power and glory to establish the eternal kingdom of God.

Much of the attractiveness of doing this sort of calculation arises from feelings that the world is getting worse instead of better, and that wickedness is increasing, and a conviction that there's no hope of things getting better when the bad people seem to outnumber God's people. That sense of alienation and fear and weariness with fighting what seems like a futile battle for righteousness is what leads to a fascination with the end of the world. The tragic and violent end of the Branch Davidian cult in Waco, Texas, came about, in part, because of the cult's obsession with the sense that the world was soon coming to an end.

If we were to be asked for a favorite or familiar passage of scripture, I daresay that none of us here would name any of the lessons we've heard this morning. They're a bit strange, aren't they, to say the least. All of them in one way or another, have the end of the world in view.

The prophet Malachi declares his vision of the final day of the Lord, "See, the day is coming, burning like an oven" (Malachi 4:1), and he describes that day as being both a day of judgment and of salvation. For the wicked it will come as judgment. For the righteous, it will be the rising of the "sun of righteousness with healing in its wings" (Malachi 4:2). Same day. But how it is experienced will be determined by the character of those who experience it. For those who live heedlessly, selfishly, unmindful of God, disobedient to God's will, it will be experienced as a "burning oven," in which all that is not good will perish. For those who live in faithfulness to God, who do God's will rather than their own, it will come as a day of salvation and blessing and healing.

In the community of Christians in Thessalonica, there were those who became so convinced that the time was short, that they figured, what's the point of continuing to work. We'll just stay in church all day, we'll join in the covered-dish suppers, we'll sing hymns, we'll pray together, we'll have good fellowship and enjoy ourselves while we wait for Jesus to come back and deliver us from this evil world.

But the writer of the epistle sharply reprimands them for this attitude, "Keep away from believers who are living in idleness and not according to the tradition they received from us" (2 Thessalonians 3:6), he tells them. He's not speaking about lazy people in general. He's speaking particularly to people who, probably because they were lazy people to begin with, are using the hope of the soon return of Christ as an excuse to stop working and sponge off the rest of the Christian community. He exhorts them to straighten up, get back to work, and follow his own example and teaching which was, "If you don't work, you don't eat." And his concluding remark on this subject is "Brothers and sisters, do not be weary in well-doing" (2 Thessalonians 3:13) — in doing what is right.

In our gospel, we find Jesus saying something very similar to his followers. In Luke's community, there were apparently some who misinterpreted the hard times they were going through, especially the persecutions that sometimes broke out against the Christians as they strove for official recognition and tolerance as a bona fide religion in the eyes of the Roman imperial power. But Luke is concerned that they not interpret a time of severe trial as a sign of the imminent end, and just give up hope and give up their mission of spreading the Gospel of Christ. So in his story, we see Jesus warning his followers that they should not interpret their troubles or the world's troubles as signs that the end is upon them. Rather, he tells them, "This will be an opportunity for you to testify . . . I will give you words and a wisdom that none of your opponents will be able to withstand or contradict. It's true that some of you will suffer betrayal by family and friends, and some of you will even be put to death. But don't worry, not a hair of your heads will be harmed."

Easy for him to say. Don't you just love the absurdity of that statement, "Some of you will be put to death, but don't worry because not a hair of your heads will be harmed"? Of course it's easy for him to say, if you take those words as the words of the risen Jesus to his church. For the risen Jesus has experienced that very paradoxical, seemingly absurd truth. He was put to death, but death did not ultimately harm him.

God raised him from the dead, the God whose word creates life where there is no life. So viewed from this side of Jesus' resurrection, those words contain, not an absurdity, but a profound truth. The follower of Jesus is someone who can be faithful, even in the face of death, because he or she knows that even death can work no ultimate harm.

Now, most of us aren't sitting around thinking about the second coming of Christ all the time like those early Christians in Luke's community or in Thessalonica. If, after nearly 2,000 years, no one has successfully calculated the date of the second advent, it's probably because we were never intended to occupy ourselves with such pursuits in the first place. To ask when or how is to ask the wrong question. But some of us may have fallen into the opposite error of thinking that because we cannot calculate the day and the hour of the end, or because the end hasn't come in all this time, there isn't any end at all. And that's a more deadly error than the error of focusing on the when and the how.

For if the New Testament is clear on anything, it is that the end has already begun. It began when God raised Jesus from the dead and exalted him as Lord of all. The completion of the end will come in God's good time, a time we cannot calculate, but which is nevertheless guaranteed. Jesus' resurrection is the first installment, the down-payment if you will, of the full re-creation of the world.

So the question for us is not "When will that day come?" nor "What will be the manner of its coming?" nor even "Will it ever come at all?" but rather "In view of the certainty of that day's coming, how should we live?"

And the answer to that question is to live in faithfulness to God. Our scripture passages agree on that answer. In faithfulness to God. In obedience to God's will. In bearing faithful witness before "kings and governors" for Jesus' sake. It is not becoming weary in doing what is right.

But that's just the rub, isn't it? It's not that we dispute the answer. We all know the answer. We've known it for as long as we've been Christians most of us. We don't doubt it. We know that we're to be faithful, to be righteous, to do what is right, to do good. And if we're mature Christians, we know also that we can't do good without the power of the Holy Spirit working within us to give us both the will and the ability to do what is right. Our doing what is right is not our achievement, but Christ's achievement within us and through us. That's what grace is: God giving to us what we need to do what God requires us to do, quite apart from any achievement or qualification of our own.

But the problem for many of us is that we get weary in well-doing. We get tired. It's hard to be faithful all the time, isn't it? It's tough to always pay attention to the needs of others more than we pay attention to our own needs and wants. It's tough to volunteer to staff a homeless shelter or feed the hungry or teach at Bible club for children from the housing projects, or to serve faithfully on the administrative board or to teach a Sunday school class and to keep on doing it week after week after week, year after year after year. It's tough, not only to give our time and energy to do these things which we know are right, but to be expected to pay for the privilege of doing them as well. It's burn-out city.

It's also tough to always try to do what is right even in our personal lives and within our families, isn't it? It's really hard to be honest all the time when it seems like we'd get ahead faster if we cut some corners. It's tough to be charitable to colleagues who'd just as soon stick a knife in our backs as not. It's hard to be committed to the causes and practices that we know are right, when it seems like we're fighting an uphill battle. We get tired. I know I do. And my family knows I do. And my friends know I do. They often pay the price when I'm tired. They get short answers, the defensive reactions, the irritable response. Maybe if we always get stroked and rewarded for doing what is right, it wouldn't be so bad, but as those disciples of Jesus discovered, they were more likely to be persecuted. Wouldn't it be so much easier to avoid becoming weary in well-doing if we could look forward to a pat on the back instead of a kick in the behind for our efforts? Or what's even worse, just taken for granted. To a group of conscientious and overworked people, the exhortation, "Do not be weary in well-doing," just adds another burden to our already over-burdened lives.

But it's just at the point of our weariness, just at the point where we're ready to quit, where our energy is all used up and burned out, that we need that vision of the approaching end to sustain us. Just as a long-distance runner needs to keep the image of the finish line in her mind in order to summon up the stamina to finish the race, or a woman in labor needs to keep her mind on the new life to come to enable her to endure her travail, so we need the truth of the second advent to enable us to run our race with patience and hope and endurance. It's not yet quitting time. The road is long, the way is hard, we will get tired to the point of exhaustion, but the end is in view, Christ is the Lord of history, and in God's good time, the end will come — an end that is really a new beginning. We may not be able to see the future in detail, but we can see the large outlines. That future means life from the dead, for us and for the whole creation. That future means that ultimately human greed and human evil and human selfishness will not have the last word. Paul says, "We are saved in hope." And he's exactly right. Not hope that is mere wishful thinking, but hope that is anchored in a firm trust in the God who raised Jesus from the dead, and who keeps his promise to his creation. That's why we must never, never lose sight of the end, that day of which the prophet Malachi, and Jesus, and Paul all spoke. They themselves lived in light of that day, and it colored all that they did and suffered and endured. It was their polestar, the fixed point by which they navigated. And it's the fixed point by which we must navigate as well if we are not to become weary in well-doing. Only hope in the final triumph of God will enable us to keep on doing what is right, despite the weariness we often feel.

How do we get that hope and keep it alive? Through prayer and worship. We must develop and nurture the habits of prayer, of relationship with God, of reflection on the scriptures. For it is out of that relationship that the vision of the day of the Lord will become real. The old saints referred to their times of prayer as "recollection of the soul." Literally, we re-collect ourselves when we become fragmented and harried and burned out. In prayer, we pull all the scattered bits of ourselves, all the depleted energies back together and become whole again.

Martin Luther, the great reformer of the church back in the 16th century, made the comment one morning when he got out of bed that his work load that day was so heavy, that he knew he would never get it all done unless he spent three hours in prayer first. Many of us find it difficult to set aside 15 minutes a day for prayer, let alone three hours, but then, not many of us are having the impact on the world that Martin Luther did either. It was in his prayer that all his energies were collected, and his action became focused and effective.

What was true of Luther has been true of all those who have been effective and faithful servants of Christ. Who can imagine the incredible success of the early Methodist movement without the disciplined prayer life of John Wesley and the early Methodist class meetings where people gathered to pray, to worship, to encourage and exhort one another in love? Wesley once wrote to a young preacher who was suffering from burn-out, "O begin! Fix some time every day to read the scriptures and to pray. It is for your life. Without this all else would be trifling and idleness." The list could go on and on. All who have been faithful witnesses and seemingly tireless in doing what is right have been sustained and inspired by their hope in God's new creation, and for all of them, that vision has been kept alive by a regular and disciplined habit of prayer.

But it is not only our personal prayer which is essential: None of us can find sufficient strength for the work by ourselves. Faith and hope are found in community. By joining together in the corporate praise of God, in worship, we re-envision the world. In worship, we deny that money or power or violence of death rule the world, and we declare that God is the real ruler. In our liturgy, our hymns, our prayers of intercession, our listening and responding to the proclaimed word, we discover a new framework for understanding who we are and what we're about. And in this community solidarity, we discover hope and a new source of energy to overcome our world-weariness and continue doing what is right. Prayer and worship are our weapons against burn-out.

Are you feeling tired and burned out trying to always do what is right? Are you weary in well-doing? Or is your hope in God's future, nurtured in prayer and worship, sustaining you and bringing to you the power of the Spirit to enable you to be a faithful witness to Jesus Christ? The prophet Isaiah has expressed this hope and confidence perhaps more beautifully than anyone else:

> *Have you not known? Have you not heard?*
> *The Lord is the everlasting God,*
>   *the Creator of the ends of the earth.*
> *He does not faint or grow weary;*
> *He gives power to the faint,*
>   *and strengthens the powerless.*
> *Even youths will faint and be weary,*
>   *and the young will fall exhausted.*
> *But those who wait in hope for the Lord will renew*
>   *their strength.*
> *They will mount up with wings like eagles,*
> *They will run and not be weary,*
> *They will walk and not faint.*
>
> *— Isaiah 40:28-31*

Thanksgiving Day
Luke 17:11-19

The Bread That Endures

Perhaps you did something this morning that many others do each morning as well — you had a piece of toast or a bagel for breakfast. Perhaps you put strawberry jam or honey on your toast and spread some cream cheese on your bagel. Around the world, this simple human ritual is repeated in a variety of ways. In Malaysia, that same piece of toast might be smeared with *kaya*, a thick jam made from coconut milk. In Taiwan or in Beijing, instead of toast, it may be a steamed bun filled with bits of roast pork and vegetables. In India, the morning ritual includes rolling out some simple whole wheat dough into flat round chapatis. In France, those wonderful flaky croissants will tantalize many palates first thing in the morning. The old saying about bread being the "staff of life" is not merely a cliché. It's true. There's probably no more universal food than bread. Since human beings first learned to cultivate grains, they have been grinding that grain into flour or meal and baking bread.

Perhaps that's why baking bread is such a satisfying activity. Not only is the aroma of baking bread one of life's great olfactory pleasures, but baking bread is an activity that is fundamental to human life, and doing it links us with something very basic. Perhaps if we could get the leaders of the various warring communities together in a kitchen to bake bread, some of the prejudices and ancient animosities which result in so much violence would be dissipated. It's hard to think violent thoughts when your arms are elbow-deep in flour.

It's little wonder then that bread has become a metaphor for life itself. Not only in English, but in many languages, bread symbolizes life. So we don't need to strain our minds too hard to understand what Jesus means when he says, in our gospel lesson, "I am the Bread of Life. Whoever comes to me will never be hungry and whoever believes in me will never be thirsty." We know immediately what he means. And perhaps just because his meaning is so clear, we skip right over it without giving it much thought. Hardly any statement in the Bible is more transparently obvious. And yet, as John shows us, those to whom that statement was spoken didn't understand it nearly so readily. Perhaps its meaning is not quite as transparent as it seems at first glance, or perhaps one has to be in a certain condition in order to understand it.

The obvious meaning of Jesus' words are that, like bread, he is the one who gives and sustains life. He nourishes the eater. Just as physical bread sustains the life of the body, so Jesus sustains the life of the spirit. To come to Jesus or to believe in him is to live life as it was meant to be lived, to know life in its richest and fullest sense.

Yet so many people seem to miss out on life in that full and rich sense. Why? Possibly it's because so many have a distorted understanding of bread. If Jesus uses bread as a metaphor for the deeper dimensions of life, we have often done just the reverse. In our colloquial speech, bread does not refer to the deeper aspects of life, but to material things, specifically to money. When the teenager comes to his father and says, "Dad, I need some bread," he's not asking for his dad's wise counsel. He's not even asking for a peanut butter and jelly sandwich. When we see someone whiz by us in a new BMW, we say, "Wouldn't it be nice to have the bread for one of those?" Our figures of speech betray our understanding of reality and our true values. For us the staff of life is money. Money is what makes life both possible and worth living. We have twisted the philosopher Descarte's statement, "I think; therefore I am," into "I buy; therefore I am."

We're not the first people in history to confuse our metaphors and therefore, confuse our values. The prophet Isaiah chided the people of Israel, "Why do you spend your money for that which is not bread, and your labor for that which does not satisfy?" (Isaiah 55:2). And in our passage today, we hear Jesus saying to his disciples, "Do not work for the bread which perishes, but for the bread which endures to eternal life." There has always been a temptation for people to think that material things and physical reality are the only things that are real. It's so much easier to concentrate on what we can see and touch than it is to deal with the more intangible, though no less real, aspects of life. It's easier to surround ourselves with gadgets and gizmos that make noise and entertain us than it is to take the journey inward to silence and solitude where we meet God at the center of our beings. We do spend our substance on that which is not really bread and labor for that which does not really satisfy.

The strange thing is that, deep down inside, we really know that focussing on material things does not really satisfy the sharpest hungers of our souls. Not many of us are under the illusion that our deepest yearnings can be satisfied by the things we buy. We know instinctively and intuitively that when Jesus says "One does not live by bread alone, but by every word which comes from the mouth of God," he is absolutely correct. We know, too, that Frederick Buechner is correct when he writes that when we eat bread we acknowledge our dependence, not only on food for our physical life, but on God and on others, for the emptiness of our bellies reminds us of other kinds of emptiness which not even the blue plate special can fill.

And yet, almost as though we can't help ourselves, we keep striving to get more and more material things, more and more money, *as though* those things could fill up the spiritual and emotional hungers of our souls. We neglect the life of the spirit, we avoid prayer, we avoid intimacy with others, we run away from ourselves, from God, from the living Bread which gives eternal life.

If one danger is that we ignore our need for spiritual bread in favor of the bread which does not satisfy, another related, and equally deadly, danger is that we try to satisfy both our material and spiritual hungers, but keep them completely separate from each other. It is very easy for us to break our life into little compartments. In one compartment we keep our job. Whatever we do at work, whatever decisions we have to make, the language we use in the office or shop floor, stays in that little box labelled work. In another compartment we have our pleasures. And we pursue these as though they are unrelated to anything else in our lives. Another compartment is labelled home and family, and we behave in certain ways that may be very different from the way we behave at work or at the football stadium. A fourth compartment is labelled religion or church, and we're a different person there too. We give God a certain portion of ourselves, our time, our money, and our energies. But we keep God confined within that box labelled religion. We don't allow God to get in the box labelled job or pleasure or family. We "have" our religion the same way that we "have" season tickets to the New York Giants games or a new Toyota.

This ability to compartmentalize our lives leads inevitably to the absurd situation where people who claim to be good Christians can surround themselves with every material comfort money can buy and, at the same time, feel little or no responsibility for their homeless neighbors on the streets of their city or for their neighbors dying of starvation in the Sudan, or even for their hurting neighbor across the street who's just gone through a painful divorce or is struggling with a life-threatening illness. Oh, to be sure, we sometimes feel compassion, and even sometimes give money to various world hunger projects or other worthy causes. But we don't really ever get to the point of breaking down the walls between the compartments in our lives in order to see that our confession of Christ is the center which organizes and controls every aspect of our lives, whether it be our life at work or at home or at play. By keeping all the compartments separate, we can be as spiritual as we want to be, but our spirituality will be a private and personal thing without any necessary connection to any other area of our lives.

But as Jesus' statements about bread make clear, our physical or material life and our spiritual life are inseparable. Any attempt to separate them results in a distortion. Much of the meaning of our sacrament of holy communion is to be found just at this point. We are reminded graphically of the wholeness of our lives, of how deeply dependent we are for both spiritual and physical life upon the grace of God in Jesus Christ. The bread which we eat at the Lord's table is real bread. It's flour and water and salt. It reminds us of the basic necessity of food for our bodies. Eating bread ties us intimately to all other human beings for whom bread is the staff of life. It also reminds us that in Jesus Christ, God took on real flesh and blood, thereby forever sanctifying the material world. At the same time, this bread of the sacrament also has a transcendent meaning. It conveys to us the very presence of Christ himself. It is Christ's body. He is our bread. His life is meditated to us so that our life transcends the merely physical and begins to partake of that quality of life which belongs to God — eternal life.

Mortimer Arias, a Methodist bishop in Bolivia, tells a story which graphically brings home to us the meaning of the bread of life. He was at a worship service in a rural area of the country, but there was no church building. The service was being held in a large tent. Bishop Arias was celebrating the sacrament of the Lord's supper. Among the crowd of people coming to the front to receive the elements, he noticed a barefoot boy about 11 years old. When the plate with the tiny pieces of bread passed in front of him, instead of taking one piece as is customary, he began grabbing whole handfuls of bread and eating it hungrily. It was then that Bishop Arias realized that this little boy from this poor area of Bolivia really was hungry. For him the bread at communion was not just a spiritual symbol. It was, in reality, the staff of life. The bishop said that he suddenly understood the sacrament of the Lord's supper in an entirely new way. He understood God's intention for the wholeness and connectedness of life.

When we recover that sense of the wholeness and integration of both spiritual and material aspects of life, we will be able to celebrate Thanksgiving in a much deeper way. Our feasting on the stuffed turkey and all the fixings of our traditional dinner will not be simply another orgy of over-eating, but a reminder of how deeply dependent we are on the Bread of Heaven for life itself, and of how deeply connected we are with every other person, and particularly those for whom bread is a luxury. When we begin to allow the hungers of our bellies and the hungers of our souls to be integrated, then we will discover a connection to the compassion of God that will enable us to become broken bread and poured out wine for others, that they too might find the Bread of Life.

The Feast Of Christ The King
Luke 23:35-43

Pleased To Reconcile

Did you ever secretly wish that we had kings and queens here in America? I think that must be a secret wish of many of us, if the tabloid newspapers and magazines which are always on sale at the supermarket checkout counters are any indication. Between the romantic antics of Hollywood and the goings-on of the British royal family, the tabloids do a rushing business. (I won't embarrass any of us by asking how many secretly enjoy reading those tabloids as we're standing in line.) There's hardly a week goes by that there isn't some story about the latest marital couplings among the British royals. From all appearances, poor Queen Elizabeth, like her illustrious and straitlaced grandmother, Queen Victoria, is definitely not amused. Personally, I think the British royal family is worth every penny they're paid for the service they perform in keeping the media, and therefore the public attention, focussed on them, leaving the government free to get on with its business. Although it's unlikely we'll get a royal family for ourselves, we do seem to be in love with the idea of royalty.

The final Sunday of the Christian year is The Feast of Christ the King. It's fitting to conclude the liturgical year with an acclamation of the royalty of Christ, though we do this much more frequently than once a year. The sovereignty of Christ is well-affirmed in our hymns and in the language we use to speak about Jesus in our worship. In a few weeks, we'll be singing "Come and worship, come and worship, worship Christ the newborn king," and "Hark! the herald angels sing, glory to the newborn king," as we celebrate Christmas.

But as often as we use the language of royalty in our praise of Christ, I wonder if we really have a good understanding of what we mean when we hail Jesus as a king, and what, if anything, the kingship of Jesus has to do with our lives. Those two questions, it seems to me, are ones we have to consider seriously: What does it mean to confess Jesus as King, and what personal significance does that confession have for us?

Both our epistle and gospel refer to Jesus as king. In the gospel, the term is overlaid with heavy irony. It is Jesus' executioners, the Roman soldiers, who use the term in their mocking taunt: "If you are the King of the Jews, save yourself." The clear implication is that if Jesus is a king, then kingship doesn't mean much. Even the inscription written over his head, "This is the King of the Jews," is clearly meant as a final insult to this one who wears a crown, not of gold and precious gems, but of thorns, and whose throne is not a stately seat of power, but a rough wooden cross on which he is hung up to die. So much for all would-be royal pretenders!

Yet Luke paints for us a portrait of one who, even as he is dying, and even as he is cruelly mocked by the perverse titles and trappings of royalty, nevertheless acts like a king in his dying moments. One of the criminals who has been crucified with him suddenly is overcome by remorse and a keen feeling that this man on the next cross is a victim of cruel injustice, while he is getting no more than he deserves, and in his own agony, he says, "Jesus, remember me when you come into your kingdom." And Jesus replies with the calm authority of a true king, "Truly I tell you, today you will be with me in Paradise."

If we leave this narrative of Jesus' crucifixion with its ironic mockery, and turn to the epistle passage from Colossians, we find what appears to be a hymn-like paean of praise to Christ which employs some of the most exalted language in the

New Testament. This truly is praise for a king, and not the ironic taunts of enemies or executioners. Listen to the phrases: "the image of the invisible God, the firstborn of all creation ... the head of the body, the church, the firstborn from the dead ... in him all the fullness of God was pleased to dwell" (Colossians 1:15, 18-19). That's language fit for royalty, isn't it? This is more like it, we think. This is language we can sink our teeth into and take pride in. We who are followers of Jesus can relate to language like this.

Unfortunately, down through the centuries, the church has often let these magnificent cadences of praise lead it into triumphalism. In the name of Christ the King, or the Pantocrator as he was called in the early church (meaning "Ruler of the Universe"), the church militant has often trampled its enemies, conquered and converted people by the sword, and imposed both spiritual and temporal rule over people through the use of terror.

And yet, it is not these wonderful praises from Colossians which are to be blamed; rather it is the church's failure to read them closely enough. For the author has not contented himself with this majestic and exalted praise of Christ. He has not left the door open to the kind of triumphalism to which Christians have often succumbed. He has clearly anchored these praises to the concrete event of Jesus' death on the cross. "Through him, God was pleased to reconcile all things, whether on earth or in heaven, by making peace through the blood of his cross" (Colossians 1:20). This is the sentence that qualifies and defines the meaning of all those high-sounding praises. This is the sentence that illuminates what it means to be the image of the invisible God, the firstborn of all creation, and so on. The majestic and glorious king of heaven is none other than the one who "made peace through the blood of his cross."

What Luke has done narratively to show us what kind of a king Jesus is, the author of Colossians has done theologically. Luke shows us a dying Jesus reconciling a penitent criminal. The writer of Colossians shows us the God whose saving plan to reconcile all things in earth and heaven stands behind, and is carried out through, that same dying Jesus.

If history did not tell the story, who would believe that, nearly 2,000 years after an obscure Galilean peasant, who gained some local notoriety as a wandering preacher and healer, and was executed by the Romans who were very touchy about any perceived threat to their imperial domination, there would not be a single nation in the world where this obscure peasant was not worshipped and acclaimed as a king, a king whose kingdom shall never end, and who by his power holds the universe together? Fantastic, isn't it! Where in this world can one go and not discover somewhere a group of people who confess Jesus as Lord and King? In countries rich and poor, large and small, with repressive or democratic governments, the church which Christ has gathered into one body, and of which he is the head, is present and growing.

In the highlands of the interior of the East Malaysian state of Sarawak on the heavily-forested island of Borneo, there is a small village called Barrio. It is only accessible by small planes capable of landing on the tiny mountain-ringed runway, or by a long journey by canoes up jungle rivers and trekking on foot. And yet, every person in that village confesses the Lordship of Jesus Christ. In southern Zaire, where political turmoil and corrupt government has many people on the brink of starvation, there are small groups of Christians who gather in rural mud-brick churches, sometimes without even a roof, and there each Sunday, they sing the praises of a king whose name is Jesus. Through the long years of repression in the Soviet Union and its satellites, and in China where for so many years public worship was forbidden, we now discover in this era when the walls of repression are falling that the church was not only alive but growing, and is now stronger than it ever was in those lands. Many people in those lands refused to confess Mao Tse-Tung or Stalin or Brezhnev as king, preferring to confess Jesus as king instead, sometimes at great personal cost.

Somehow, that historical development — the universal reign of One who died as a subversive criminal at the town dump of Jerusalem nearly 2,000 years ago — must be explained. It certainly cannot be explained by the misguided attempts of the church to impose that rule by force or intimidation down through the centuries. All those attempts have ended in ruinous failure. Nor was it merely the power of the ideas which Jesus proclaimed, though those ideas are powerful, and have undoubtedly shaped lives and nations. Something more is at work here.

In his marvelous series of children's books called *The Chronicles of Narnia,* C. S. Lewis tells stories of the imaginary land of Narnia and the king who rules it, a king whose name is Aslan. Aslan is a lion, the Great Lion, at whose roar the very trees of the forest tremble in awe.

In the first book of the series, four human children are playing in an old wardrobe when they suddenly discover that it is a doorway to Narnia. Narnia, at this junction in its history, is under the spell of a wicked witch whose rule is evil and oppressive. The youngest child, Lucy, gives the best description of Narnia under the witch's rule: "It's always winter, but never Christmas." The children enter into a plot to overthrow the power of the witch, since they hear from some of the inhabitants a rumor that Aslan the rightful king is returning. One of the children, however, the younger boy Edmund, is a spoiled brat, and when he discovers that he can't have everything his way, he betrays the other animals and his brother and sisters to the witch, and they fall into her clutches.

In the climactic scene, the witch comes to Aslan and tells him that according to the deep magic from the dawn of time, she is entitled to have the blood of anyone who is a traitor. So she demands to be allowed to sacrifice Edmund on the Stone Table, a large ritual stone that has always been in Narnia. Aslan acknowledges the justice of her claim, but then offers to become the victim of the sacrifice himself in place of Edmund.

The witch, of course, is delighted at this offer, for she not only gets the blood she demands, but gets rid of her ancient enemy and arch-rival Aslan at the same time. Before the horrified eyes of the children, Aslan allows himself to be bound, humiliated, and slaughtered on the Stone Table to the triumphant howls of the witch. The two girls Susan and Lucy stay all night by his body, grieving their loss, for now it is obvious the wicked witch has won, and her rule over Narnia will be secure.

But at sunrise, when they walk away a short distance to stretch their legs, they suddenly hear a gigantic crack, and when they look around, the Stone Table is split from end to end and the body of Aslan is gone. Suddenly they hear his voice, and there in the morning sunlight he stands alive and more majestic than ever!

When they express their delight and their surprise, Aslan tells them that the witch knew the deep magic from the dawn of time, but that there is a deeper magic which she did not know. Her knowledge only went back to the dawn of time, he says.

> *But if she could have looked a little further back into the stillness and darkness before Time, she would have read there a different incantation. She would have known that when a willing victim who had committed no treachery is killed in a traitor's stead, the Table would crack, and Death itself would start working backward.*[1]

That's what the writer of Colossians is getting at when he mentions the blood of Jesus' cross in the same breath as the images of the exalted, cosmic Christ. That's what Luke is getting at when he tells us in story fashion of a man who in his dying agony can find it within himself to royally pronounce forgiveness and reconciliation to a penitent criminal. That old cross at the town dump of Jerusalem was, in reality, the symbol of kingly power that had its origins far back in "the deeper magic from before the dawn of time." It was the power that started death working backward. So Jesus became "the first-born from the dead," the first in a long series of men and women over whom death can never again hold ultimate power to destroy. Those who confess this dying man on the cross as king are "transferred from the kingdom of darkness to the kingdom of God's beloved Son." Those who confess him as king are people for whom the crown of thorns and the nails and the cross of shame are emblems of a royal power the likes of which the world has never seen before or since, and which is greater than the mightiest armies, the richest corporations, the most destructive thermonuclear warheads, or the most thorough political revolutions. His royal power is the power of suffering love, of sacrifice, of faith in the power of God to raise the dead, and that power is the supreme power in heaven and earth.

So, then, what does it mean to us personally to confess Jesus as king? Is it anything more than high-sounding words that we sing in hymns or affirm in our liturgy? That depends on the extent to which we commit ourselves to the lordship of Jesus. Whatever we commit ourselves to is what determines our behavior and shapes our lives. It follows then, that if we commit ourselves to Jesus as king, then the definition of kingship he lived out will determine the way we live under that kingship. If his kingship is defined by his sacrificial death for others on the cross, then our lives will be cross-shaped as well.

This means that in our relationships with other people, we take our king's way of conducting ourselves. His way was to forgive and reconcile a penitent criminal. Our way, then, can do no less than be forgiving and reconciling. His way was to give himself willingly for others; our way can do no less than be self-giving for the benefit of others as well. If our lives had sufficient value to him that he would die for us, then we must place no less value on ourselves than he did. This means, among other things, that we do not abuse our bodies with substances that are destructive, we do not abuse ourselves or others with exploitative sexual behavior. We resolve to be the best persons we can be with the help of his grace. In that way, we honor his trust in us.

If Jesus is king, he is king not only in the personal sphere of individual integrity and relationships with other people. He is king of the whole universe, and therefore, that lordship must be acknowledged and confessed in our relationships to the earth itself. We have to stop seeing ourselves as owners and begin confessing that we are stewards of the creation. So we will exercise that stewardship conscientiously, repenting of our wasteful and polluting behavior, husbanding the earth's resources instead of exploiting them for the single motive of profit.

In short, there is no area of our lives to which the king's authority does not extend. Nothing can be withheld from our confession of Jesus as Lord and king. If he is sovereign at all, he must and will be sovereign of all. And the way we live in our personal lives, our business dealings, our social and family relationships, our lives as citizens and keepers of the earth — all will testify to whose kingdom we have pledged our allegiance.

---

1. Lewis, C.S., *The Lion, The Witch And The Wardrobe,* (Collier Books: New York, New York, 1970), p. 160.

www.ingramcontent.com/pod-product-compliance
Lightning Source LLC
Chambersburg PA
CBHW051049160426
43193CB00010B/1116